In Other Words

PHRASES FOR GROWTH MINDSET

A Teacher's Guide to Empowering Students
through Effective Praise and Feedback

Annie Brock and Heather Hundley

Published in the United States by:
Ulysses Press
P.O. Box 3440
Berkeley, CA 94703
www.ulyssespress.com

ISBN13: 978-1-61243-791-0
Library of Congress Control Number: 2018930754

Printed in Canada by Marquis Book Printing
10 9 8 7 6 5 4

Acquisitions editor: Casie Vogel
Managing editor: Claire Chun
Editor: Shayna Keyles
Proofreader: Renee Rutledge
Indexer: Sayre Van Young
Front cover design: what!design @ whatweb.com
Cover art: speech bubbles © Vladgrin/shutterstock.com

CONTENTS

SECTION ONE

INTRODUCTION

OVERVIEW OF THE GROWTH MINDSET

In 2006, Dr. Carol Dweck, the Lewis and Virginia Eaton Professor of Psychology at Stanford University, published a book called *Mindset* that changed the way many educators, including us, approached student learning. Armed with an aggregation of 30 year's research, Dweck outlined a powerful theory on the two mindsets she had uncovered in her research subjects—fixed mindset and growth mindset.

Dweck's journey began while she was studying how students coped with failure. She realized that students tended to handle failure in one of two ways: Some seemed to thrive in the face of a challenge, while others did their best to avoid challenging situations. She noted that students willing to grapple with a difficult problem tended to have better overall academic outcomes than those who practiced avoidance techniques. The more she looked, the more she realized that the mindset with which a person approached a situation made a tremendous difference in the

2

outcome of that situation. She named the two mindsets fixed mindset and growth mindset.[1]

FIXED MINDSET: The belief that we are born with a fixed amount of intelligence and ability.

GROWTH MINDSET: The belief that with practice, perseverance, and effort, people have limitless potential to learn and grow.

Fixed Mindset	Growth Mindset
Belief that ability and talent are fixed or limited; that one will likely not significantly improve in an area if one does not demonstrate natural talent in that area.	Belief that success is a direct result of effort put forth, rather than one's natural ability or talent.
Tendency to avoid challenges in order to avoid failure or appearing incompetent.	Tendency to approach challenges without fear of failure.
Tendency to give up after encountering an obstacle.	Willingness to try a new strategy when hitting an obstacle.
Tendency to blame others or underlying circumstances for failure.	Tendency to view failures and mistakes as stepping stones to more successful outcomes.
Rarely identifies lack of effort as the cause of failure.	Ability to readily identify the link between effort and achievement.
Tendency to shut down in the face of mistakes.	Tendency to be energized by failure as an opportunity to grow and overcome a problem.

Fixed Mindset	Growth Mindset
Views mistakes as an embarrassment, not a learning opportunity.	Demonstrates understanding that mistakes are a part of the learning process.
Tendency to view feedback as criticism and/or a personal attack.	Tendency to seek feedback as a necessary ingredient for growth.

Here's the thing about the mindsets: Both fixed mindset and growth mindset exist in us all. It's whether we choose to view various situations through the lens of the growth mindset or the fixed mindset that makes all the difference. In *Mindset*, Dweck points out that all people begin life with a growth mindset. Indeed, babies are the very picture of the growth mindset. They don't care if what they are saying makes sense as they are navigating learning to speak, and no matter how often they fall in the pursuit of learning to walk, they always get back up.[2] So, the question becomes, at what point do fixed mindsets begin to develop? Some would argue that fixed-mindset tendencies begin to emerge in childhood.

Dweck writes of raising children to have a growth mindset: "If parents want to give their children a gift, the best thing they can do is to teach their children to love challenges, be intrigued by mistakes, enjoy effort, and keep on learning. That way, their children don't have to be slaves of praise. They will have a lifelong way to build and repair their own confidence."[3]

Much in the same way, teachers can offer students the gift of pursuing challenges, working through mistakes, and learning there is a direct line leading from effort to growth. In this book, we seek to give educators the tools to communicate with students, create Growth-mindset classroom atmospheres, and provide praise and feedback in a way that fosters growth mindsets.

ABOUT THE BOOK

This book is meant to be a shorthand guide to communicating with students. Much of what is written here has been adapted from our longer works on the topic of growth mindset—*The Growth Mindset Coach* and *The Growth Mindset Playbook*. Consider this a primer of sorts, a cheat-sheet version of *Playbook* and *Coach* filled with tips, strategies, and go-to phrases designed to help teachers shift their thoughts, words, and deeds into the growth-mindset zone.

When it comes to praise and feedback, many parents and teachers fall into the same fixed-mindset traps that can ultimately hamper children's ability to develop growth mindsets. When we say well-meaning things like, "You're so smart!" we are overlooking the fact that those words—words that are associated with personal attributes—may ultimately be damaging. "You're so smart," might feel like appropriate praise in the moment, but later when the student meets with inevitable failure, they may fall to pieces because the words they internalized about themselves—you're so smart—don't seem so true, after all.

In our book, *The Growth Mindset Coach*, we differentiated between person praise and process praise, and we gave tips to teachers for providing feedback in a way that helped students see that academic success is about overcoming obstacles, putting forth effort, and turning mistakes into learning opportunities. In this book, in addition to offering a primer on growth-oriented praise and feedback, we'll delve into methods to maximize growth-mindset communication in various school relationships, examine the ways that the two mindsets may play a role in the school day, and introduce you to the tools you need to respond to situations with a growth mindset. We'll also demonstrate how you can create conditions in your relationships, classroom, and school in which the growth mindsets of others will have the opportunity to flourish. The sections of this book discuss:

Self-talk: People in the fixed mindset believe they can't lose if they don't play, but what they don't realize is that they'll never win that way, either. Here, we examine how our self-talk plays a critical role in choosing our mindset as we approach situations, including offering tips and strategies for taking control of your self-talk, encouraging your growth mindset through self-talk and affirmations, and overcoming the fixed-mindset voice by recognizing triggers and using specific language to reframe a situation.

Teacher-to-student communication: This section provides strategies for infusing the growth-mindset language, both verbally and nonverbally, into your interactions with students. This section will cover establishing rich, meaningful relationships; providing growth-oriented praise and feedback; promoting shame awareness; interacting with students who routinely demonstrate negative behaviors; and more.

Peer-to-peer communication: Here, we focus on two types of peer-to-peer relationships in the school setting, and the communication that defines them. Teacher-to-teacher communication will cover strategies and tips for growth-oriented communication with colleagues, and peer-to-peer communication will focus on facilitating growth-oriented language in student-to-student interactions.

School-to-home communication: Growth-mindset efforts at school may be hampered by fixed-mindset messages at home. In this section, we'll focus on getting parents in on the growth-mindset game by offering ideas for helping parents become acquainted with growth mindset and giving tips for how to incorporate growth-mindset messaging at home.

The whole-school mindset: Not only do all people have a predominant mindset, but, in a sense, organizations do, as well. What mindset is being communicated by the policies, procedures, values, and routines of your school? In this section, we encourage education professionals to consider the ways the school organization, as a singular entity, projects a growth or fixed mindset, and how you can make efforts to help develop a growth-mindset school culture.

EXAMINING YOUR MINDSET

A person with a fixed mindset tends to believe that people are born with a fixed amount of intelligence, skill, and talent. Often, when faced with a challenging situation, those with a fixed mindset work very hard to avoid failing or looking stupid, robbing themselves of rich life experiences. Conversely, people with a growth mindset generally believe that with practice, perseverance, and effort, they have unlimited potential to learn and grow in any area. In this mindset, intelligence, skill, and talent can always be developed, if one is willing to work for it. People with growth mindsets are more inclined to tackle challenges and believe making mistakes and overcoming obstacles are integral to the process of growth.

We think it is important to understand which of the mindsets—fixed or growth—is your predominant mindset. If you've never taken a mindset assessment, it's easy. Just put a checkmark next to the statements that best describe your beliefs.

_____ 1. There are some things I am just not good at.

_____ 2. I don't mind failing. It's a chance to learn.

_____ 3. When others do better than me, it makes me feel inferior.

_____ 4. I like trying new things—even if it means getting out of my comfort zone.

_____ 5. It makes me feel successful when I show others I'm good at things.

_____ 6. When other people succeed, I feel inspired.

_____ 7. I feel good when I can do something others around me cannot.

_____ 8. It is possible to change how intelligent you are.

_____ 9. I think people are born with a certain amount of intelligence and they can't do much to change that.

_____ 10. Feeling frustrated makes me want to try harder.

In this assessment, the odd-numbered statements (1, 3, 5, 7, 9) are common attitudes of someone operating in a fixed mindset, while the even-numbered statements (2, 4, 6, 8, 10) are common of a person operating in a growth mindset. It's important to remember there are no right and wrong answers here—understanding your predominant mindset is simply the first step in developing a Growth-mindset classroom. Most likely, you have a mixture of the mindsets. Some tasks you probably approach with a growth mindset, while taking on other types of tasks triggers your fixed mindset. Regardless of your starting point, here's what we know: Your ability to grow and change in this regard depends on the amount of work you're willing to do. If you're ready to put in the work to become an authentic growth-mindset teacher, then we have no doubt you can achieve it.

MORE ABOUT THE MINDSETS

Now that you have an understanding of the two mindsets, let's examine how they might be at play in your school or classroom. Below, you'll find hypothetical examples of self-talk from the fixed- and growth-mindset perspectives; note how they have very different views of the same situations.

Fixed Mindset	Growth Mindset
My administrator marked "needs improvement" in several areas of my evaluation. I am a horrible teacher.	I need to follow up on the "needs-improvement" areas of my review with specific questions. Maybe my administrator can point me to resources to help me improve these areas of my teaching.

Fixed Mindset	Growth Mindset
Megan is bad at math. It's just not something she's good at.	How can I teach Megan math in a way that connects her to the material?
Jay can do the work, but he's not doing it. He's just lazy.	I know Jay can do the work, but he's not doing it. I need to reexamine my approach and figure out how to engage him.
Mr. Jones gets all the teaching awards and accolades because he is a total suck up and glory-seeker.	Mr. Jones gets recognized often for his teaching; I should observe him to see if I can apply some of his strategies to my own practice.
My students ruined this lesson; they just refused to cooperate.	My students didn't connect with this lesson. How could I make it more engaging for them?
This class is filled with bad kids. I heard they are completely unteachable.	I will approach this year taking each individual student into account. All students can be taught; it's a matter of finding the right approach.
Dara's parents obviously don't value education. She'll never go anywhere with a family like that.	I believe Dara's parents want what is best for her; how can I give them the tools they need to support her in a positive way?
Carl has a bad attitude and is completely checked out; he has no hope of graduating.	I should ask Carl to write down his future goals, and help him see how his choices now will make a difference.

Fixed Mindset	Growth Mindset
My students performed poorly on this test; obviously they weren't listening.	My students performed poorly on this test; obviously I need to reteach the material in a way they will understand.

Are you seeing a pattern? The fixed-mindset teacher approaches situations as unchangeable, views a difficult situation as a personal attack, and when things go wrong, it's usually someone else's fault. Now, juxtapose that with the inner monologue of a growth-mindset teacher. Compared to the fixed-mindset teacher, who is quick to give up and look for someone else to blame, the growth-mindset teacher seeks to understand the problem and find a way to solve it.

Dweck identified five key situations in which a person's mindset has a significant influence on the outcome.[4]

1) Challenges. A difficult task one might encounter.

2) Obstacles. Something that prevents progress in pursuit of a goal or achievement.

3) Effort. The work put forth in the process of completion of a task, challenge, or goal.

4) Criticism. A critical judgment from another.

5) Success of others. Achievement or success achieved by another person; particularly, coveted success.

For a person operating in the fixed mindset, the goal is almost always to appear smart and competent, and to avoid failure or embarrassment. Conversely, in the growth mindset, a person's responses to a given situation reflect a desire for genuine learning and growth, regardless of the possibility of meeting stumbling blocks or failing. Let's look at some typical fixed- and growth-mindset responses to each of the five situations Dweck defined.[5]

Facing a Challenge

FIXED MINDSET: Challenges are avoided to maintain the appearance of intelligence and capability.

GROWTH MINDSET: Challenges are embraced, demonstrating a desire to learn and grow.

Obstacles

FIXED MINDSET: Giving up in the face of obstacles and setbacks is a common response in the fixed mindset.

GROWTH MINDSET: Showing grit and resilience in the face of obstacles and setbacks is a common response in the growth mindset.

Effort

FIXED MINDSET: Putting in effort is viewed as a negative trait; if you're good at it, you shouldn't have to try hard.

GROWTH MINDSET: Putting in effort and working hard are critical to paving the way to achievement and success.

Criticism

FIXED MINDSET: Negative feedback, regardless of how constructive, is ignored and often viewed as a personal attack.

GROWTH MINDSET: Criticism isn't a personal attack, it's a tool for providing important feedback that can aid in learning and growth.

Success of Others

FIXED MINDSET: The success of others is viewed as a threat and evokes feelings of insecurity or vulnerability.

GROWTH MINDSET: The success of other people can be a source of inspiration and education.

***

Now, let's look at how these situations play out in schools. We will examine how the fixed and growth mindsets affect people we meet each day in our schools, and compare how the two mindsets make a difference in the outcomes of various common situations.

Mindsets for Teachers

Fixed	Growth
This student will never learn how to do this.	How can I present the information so the student understands or makes growth toward their learning goal?
This student hates school and there is nothing I can do to change that.	How can I engage and connect with the student using his passions and interests?
I will never be as good as that teacher.	I should ask to observe her so I can learn from her.
My administrator encourages us to incorporate new ways for students to demonstrate their learning, but I don't want to fail.	I am going to add something new each quarter. If it fails, I will be prepared to model how I can learn from the mistakes so I can improve on it the next time I try.

Mindsets for Students

Fixed	Growth
I am not good at this. I'll never get it!	I am not good at this yet. I am going to keep working at it, trying new strategies, and focusing on getting better.
I am always messing up!	I am going to look at what I did and determine what I can learn from my last attempt.
This is so easy for me.	I am going to find a way to make this more challenging.
No one in my family is good at math.	If I work hard, try new strategies, ask for help, and continue to practice, I will improve in math.

Mindsets for Administrators

Fixed	Growth
We need a policy that states students should have out-of-school suspensions when they won't comply.	Identifying the lagging skills of students who do not comply can help us craft lessons to improve their behaviors.
This problem is due to the lack of teacher buy-in and teamwork.	This problem is an opportunity to learn about our limitations, mistakes, and how we can work together as a staff.
The school culture is so negative. We will never change!	Gathering feedback from the staff and identifying problems will help us grow and do better in the future.
I don't have time to provide feedback on teacher evaluations. Besides, the teachers don't want to hear my ideas.	The feedback I provide on evaluations helps teachers reflect and develop their skills.

Mindsets for Parents

Fixed	Growth
My child is just not an athlete.	If she puts in the effort and asks her coach and teammates for some extra support, she can increase her skill.
I don't know why the teacher expects the students to correct their mistakes.	Correcting mistakes helps my child learn.
These tasks are too demanding, and he won't ever need to know how to do them.	Productive struggle helps my child build stamina for learning and improve his confidence in taking on challenges and working through obstacles.
Abe doesn't need to study for his tests because he is so smart.	I should ask Abe's teacher if she can identify more challenging tasks for him.

THE FALSE GROWTH MINDSET

Dweck has warned of what she calls the "false growth mindset" since the success of her book, *Mindset*, and the subsequent increased efforts to integrate mindset as an intervention in schools across the country. Essentially, the false growth mindset is a series of oversimplifications, misnomers, and misapplications of Dweck's mindset research.[6] So, how can we avoid the false growth mindset? Below, we offer strategies for avoiding the traps of the false growth mindset.

Oversimplification

WHAT IT LOOKS LIKE: The concept of mindset may seem simple, but mindsets are based on decades of scientific research. Many people mistakenly boil down the concept of mindset to one idea: effort. It's more than that.

HOW TO AVOID IT: Understand the research behind the mindsets. Read Dweck's book, *Mindset*. Recognize that fostering growth mindsets is more than praising effort.

The Talent Myth

WHAT IT LOOKS LIKE: People believe that the idea of natural talent and growth mindset are at odds with one another.

HOW TO AVOID IT: Growth mindset does not negate talent. Natural talent exists; growth mindset and natural talent are not mutually exclusive. Growth mindset is the concept of applying effort on top of whatever talent exists to achieve greater results.

SITUATION
Any Effort Is Good

WHAT IT LOOKS LIKE: Growth mindset is about putting in effort. It's that simple.

HOW TO AVOID IT: Well, no, it's not that simple. Growth mindset *is* about putting in effort. But that effort should result in improvement. If it doesn't, then a developed growth mindset would recognize the lack of progress and seek new strategies. Not all effort is created equal.

SITUATION
The Growth-Mindset Claim

WHAT IT LOOKS LIKE: Claiming you have a growth mindset makes it so.

HOW TO AVOID IT: While we believe self-talk is important, just saying you have a growth mindset isn't enough. You've got to walk the walk. Plus, as we've pointed out, everyone has *both* a fixed and growth mindset. Anyone who claims otherwise isn't being honest with you or themselves.

Again, we all have a mixture of fixed and growth mindsets. The first step to mastering a growth mindset is being honest with ourselves about what triggers our fixed mindsets. Growth-mindset research suggests that teaching students about growth and fixed mindsets can be a game changer. Once students learn about the mindsets and how their futures can be shaped—truly, their *brains* can be shaped—through dedicated practice, hard work, and effort, students begin to see the possibilities that exist for them. Dweck often tells a story of teaching a group of students about the mindsets and the ability to grow your own brain through practice and effort. One boy raised his hand and asked her, "You mean, I don't have to be dumb?"[7]

GROWTH MINDSET IN THE CLASSROOM ENVIRONMENT

As Dweck warns, oversimplification of growth mindset is a problem. It's not enough to create a bulletin board espousing the "power of yet" or offer a few handouts or one-off lessons about mindset. It's critical that the teacher demonstrate a growth mindset to their students each day, modeling what it looks like and how to overcome a fixed mindset.

That isn't to say the classroom aesthetic cannot play an important role in reminding the classroom stakeholders to consider mindset as an important part of learning. To that end, we suggest you make some meaningful changes to your classroom environment that make it conducive for growth-oriented learning. It is entirely possible to convey growth-mindset messaging through thoughtful choices in the display and arrangement of your classroom. Here are some ideas on how you can do it:

Student Work Displays

FIXED-MINDSET CLASSROOM: Work displayed is flawless, with no noticeable mistakes.

GROWTH-MINDSET CLASSROOM: Work displayed shows student effort—eraser marks, highlighted mistakes, and all.

Class Rules

FIXED-MINDSET CLASSROOM: A long, comprehensive list of things students are not allowed to do is posted to outline the criteria of failure.

GROWTH-MINDSET CLASSROOM: Positive classroom guidelines are posted that reinforce the growth-mindset ethos.

Furniture Arrangement

FIXED-MINDSET CLASSROOM: Desks are set in front-facing rows and not easily grouped for collaborative work.

GROWTH-MINDSET CLASSROOM: Students are situated collaboratively in groups, or in arrangements from which groups can easily be assembled. Wheeled furniture can be a great classroom addition.

Wall Displays/Decor

FIXED-MINDSET CLASSROOM: Messages like "Practice makes perfect" and "You are great!" are problematic because practice doesn't always make perfect, and not everyone is currently great at everything. Consider your messages through a growth-mindset lens; make sure they are purposeful.

GROWTH-MINDSET CLASSROOM: A favorite display we've seen is "Change your words, change your mindset" featuring growth alternatives to fixed messages. (e.g., Change "I'll never understand this," to "This challenging work is helping my brain grow.") Another great sign: "Make mistakes."

Teacher's Desk

FIXED-MINDSET CLASSROOM: Teacher's desk is in the back of the classroom, staring at the backs of student's heads; teacher is not inviting questions or interaction through eye contact and/or physical proximity.

GROWTH-MINDSET CLASSROOM: Teacher's desk is up front and easily accessible; better yet, there's no desk, and the teacher moves throughout the classroom during the lesson to physically invite questions and demonstrate availability. Teacher work is done in designated landing spaces.

Additional Spaces

FIXED-MINDSET CLASSROOM: No thought put into additional spaces; everyone is given the same desk and expected to sit and work in the same manner. No extra consideration given to different learning styles in the context of the classroom environment.

GROWTH-MINDSET CLASSROOM: Includes seating like a couch or bean bags and other flexible spaces, as well as extra whiteboard space or lapboards so students can collaborate and work out ideas, or a "quiet area" where students can use noise-canceling headphones to focus on individual tasks. The growth-mindset classroom accounts for different learning styles and paces.

Classroom Management

FIXED-MINDSET CLASSROOM: Names on the board with missing assignments published for the world to see. Behavior charts with big Xs for bad days, or red cards.

GROWTH-MINDSET CLASSROOM: Discipline is private, personal, and done with dignity. Consider a "coaching" approach to discipline in favor of a punitive approach.

***

The growth-mindset classroom environment should be a space that communicates hard work is a primary value. It should place a premium on taking risks and tackling challenges, and communicate to students that this is a safe space in which to ask questions and make mistakes. It should value challenges and the inevitable failure that comes with taking them on, and never emphasize perfection over effort.

ATTRIBUTES OF A GROWTH-MINDSET TEACHER

As you can see, there is so much more to growth mindset than just praising effort. If teachers hope to maximize the effectiveness of the mindset interventions, they must strive to present a growth mindset in the classroom every day and be honest with themselves and their students when combatting a fixed mindset. To that end, we've developed a list—though certainly not an exhaustive one—of attributes of a growth-mindset teacher.

- **Flexible.** Understanding of different needs. Not rooted in harmful education practices like utilizing rigid ability groups; meets students where they are in their learning.

- **High expectations.** Has high expectations of every student. Models those expectations through body language, verbal communication, positive reinforcement, and constructive feedback.

- **Communicative.** Offers lots of process-oriented feedback to students; students feel comfortable asking and answering questions.

- **Strong relationships.** Demonstrates caring and concern for students; knows about students' lives, interests, passions, etc.

- **Process oriented.** Understands that learning is less about the outcome and more about the process. Praises and critiques the process, not the person.

- **Values mistakes.** Normalizes mistakes and helps students value them as learning opportunities.

- **Empathetic.** Makes an effort to view challenges and struggles from a student's perspective.

- **Positive interdependence.** Establishes a community of learners working simultaneously on personal learning outcomes and group goals.

- **Equitable.** Understands the difference between equitability and equality, and works to provide learning opportunities and distribute resources in an equitable manner.

As you move through each section of this book, consider ways that you are incorporating growth mindset in your classroom each day. Examine how your relationships and communication—both verbal and nonverbal—are impacted by your mindset, and the measures you can take to manage your own fixed mindset and share your growth mindset with others.

SELF-TALK

AFFIRMATIONS

Making a concerted effort to infuse your vocabulary with growth-oriented language can help drive your thoughts to a more growth-oriented place. This includes your personal speech, colloquially known as the voice in your head. In our first book, we included a mantra for each section that could be said aloud or to the self to help reinforce the concept. We aren't foolish enough to believe all the students who have repeated our mantras blindly accepted the message, but we believe—and have seen evidence that—speaking a thing out loud gives it a certain truth.

There have been many studies done on the value of self-affirmation and the inherent benefits of reflecting on what we value about ourselves. There are three main explanations of why people benefit from self-affirmation, noted in an article in *New York Magazine's* The Cut.[8]

1. We enjoy reflecting on those things that we value.

2. When we feel threatened, self-affirmation reaffirms the things that we value about ourselves.

3. Self-affirmations can help regulate our emotions.

Interestingly, self-affirmations are more effective when you refer to yourself in the third person, as opposed to using the pronoun "I."[9] Try rephrasing affirmations to speak to yourself in the third person.

Affirmations to Begin the Day

Here are some affirmations that you can speak alone or with your class that will help you begin the day with a growth mindset:

- Today, I will work hard to embrace challenging situations.

- If I make a mistake, I will seek to learn from it.

- The effort I put in is directly related to my achievement.

- I will accept feedback as a gift that helps me learn and grow.

- I will make efforts to learn from other people today.

Affirmations to End the Day

Here are some affirmations that you can speak alone or with your class that will help you end the day with a growth mindset:

- Today, I did my best to embrace challenges in class. Tomorrow, I will do the same.

- The mistakes I made today will help me do better tomorrow.

- Today, I worked hard, and my hard work will show tomorrow.

- I will make use of the positive feedback and constructive criticism I received today.

- Today, I made an effort to learn from other people.

Affirmations for Facing a Setback

Here are some affirmations that you can speak alone or with your class that will help you deal with an obstacle that invokes your fixed mindset:

- This challenge will not get the best of me.

- I will keep attacking this problem until it is solved.

- I am a problem solver.

- I will not give up easily.

- I can do hard things.

- It's not "I can't," it's "I can't, yet."

- Constructive criticism is not an insult, it's an important tool for growth.

- There is valuable learning to be had by listening to and watching others.

FIXED VS. GROWTH MINDSET SELF-TALK

Whether we approach a situation with fixed or growth-mindset, self-talk may influence the outcome of the situation. Now that you have an understanding of the two mindsets, let's examine how they might be at play in your school or classroom. Below, you'll find hypothetical examples of self-talk from the fixed- and growth-mindset perspectives. Note how they have very different views of the same situations.

Low-Interest Mandatory Professional Development

FIXED MINDSET: Professional development is so boring; I never learn anything at these things.

GROWTH MINDSET: During professional development, I'll listen with an open mind and seek out new ideas.

Helicopter Parent

FIXED MINDSET: This parent is driving me crazy; he wants a progress update every day.

GROWTH MINDSET: This parent is very invested; I need to find a way to communicate with him productively.

Failing Student

FIXED MINDSET: This student is incapable of making gains in math.

GROWTH MINDSET: How can I present the information so the student will understand?

Successful Student

FIXED MINDSET: This student is a brilliant reader; she doesn't need my attention.

GROWTH MINDSET: I should develop enrichment opportunities so this student feels sufficiently challenged in reading instruction.

Success of Colleagues

FIXED MINDSET: Of course she was chosen to lead our department. She's such a suck up.

GROWTH MINDSET: I should talk to her about her promotion. If I want to take on a leadership role, I'll need to know what kind of experience it takes.

Failure of a Lesson

FIXED MINDSET: This lesson design was perfect; the students just aren't motivated to learn.

GROWTH MINDSET: I thought this lesson was going to be great, but obviously the kids weren't engaged. I should ask them for feedback for how I could improve it.

Negative Student Attitudes

FIXED MINDSET: This student just wants to derail my lessons. Every day I'm dealing with behaviors from him.

GROWTH MINDSET: These repeated behaviors might be a cry for help. I'm going to talk with my team to see what interventions might help meet the needs of this student.

Difficult Circumstances

FIXED MINDSET: With his poor home life, this student doesn't have a prayer of graduating.

GROWTH MINDSET: I believe this student can find success, regardless of his background.

***

Do you see how your self-talk as a teacher may affect the way you handle situations? The way we talk to ourselves about obstacles and frame situations in our heads can make a difference in how we choose to handle those situations. Whether you tackle an obstacle with a growth mindset, or avoid it or rationalize it away with a fixed mindset, has a great deal to do with how you've established the situation in your own head. So, the question becomes, how can you shut down fixed-mindset self-talk and replace it with growth-mindset self-talk? Often, using your growth mindset just means changing your self-talk. Instead of writing someone off, you seek to find ways to help them. Instead of giving up, you figure out another way to attack the problem. Instead of letting jealousy or feelings of inadequacy take center stage, you focus on how you can improve. Here are some strategies you can use to help transition your fixed-mindset self-talk into a growth orientation.

Know your triggers. Know the type of situation that sends you reeling into your fixed mindset, and prepare in advance how you'll handle it when it comes.

Recognize your fixed-mindset voice. Are you a blamer? An avoider? A rationalizer? Or all three? However your fixed-mindset voice presents itself, be prepared to recognize it and overcome it with a growth-mindset voice.

Name your fixed mindset. One idea for dealing with fixed-mindset triggers is to give your fixed mindset a name. Literally, a name—like, Pat, for example. That way, when you're tempted to approach a situation with a fixed-mindset response, you can say to it: "Not today, Pat!"

Invent a third-party to cast blame on. Carol Dweck tells a story in which she and her husband invented an invisible third-party named Maurice. When they were having an argument and absolutely needed to blame someone, they blamed Maurice.[10] After that, they could get down to solving the problem.

Add a "yet." When your self-talk turns to the fixed mindset (I can't do this!) add the word "yet" to the end of it. "I can't do this, yet," is a way to rephrase a fixed-mindset message into a growth-mindset message quickly and effectively, as the "yet" implies there exists a path to understanding and growth, if you're willing to put in the work.

SELF-TALK AND RELATIONSHIPS

Terry, a library media specialist, tells us about a time when she was struggling to connect with a student. The student was displaying a negative attitude toward Terry, as well as difficult behaviors that were a struggle to manage. Terry found herself thinking, *I just don't like this kid.* The thought that she would not like a small child scared her, so she set about changing her opinion by reframing her self-talk. She made an effort to learn about the student and make a non-school-related comment each time she saw him. She told herself stories about things she liked about him. She told herself things like, *His peers think he's really funny, and, actually, that was a pretty hilarious joke.* Or, she'd just look at him and think, *there are lots of things to love about this child.* Essentially, she adopted a "fake it 'til you make it" approach to connecting with the student. Slowly, she felt her internal attitudes start to shift. She said it was kind of like tricking herself into having positive thoughts, but it worked. Here are some ways you can use self-talk to improve your relationship with a student.

STRATEGY
Intentionally Look for the Good

WHAT IT SOUNDS LIKE: "I really like the way he defends his friends when someone else says something mean."

STRATEGY
Find Something You Have in Common

WHAT IT SOUNDS LIKE: "I notice she's wearing a Harry Potter t-shirt; I love Harry Potter, too. I'm going to mention that."

Three Positives for Every Negative

WHAT IT SOUNDS LIKE: "I am going to find three positive things to say before I have this student in class."

- I noticed…

- I like how you…

- You did a nice job…

Ask Others About What the Student Does Well or About Any Special Interests

WHAT IT SOUNDS LIKE: "I notice you have a great relationship with Timmy. What does Timmy do well in class? What are his special interests?"

Join in Some Fun Where There Are No Academic Demands Being Placed on the Child or Yourself

WHAT IT LOOKS LIKE: Play a game, have lunch together, plan a time to chat, tell a joke, seek to learn something new about the student, join in playtime at recess, or take note of favorite extracurriculars.

Ask Their Peers

WHAT IT SOUNDS LIKE: "What do you like or enjoy about your friends?"

Create a compliment circle and have students share a compliment about peers in their class. Have students share a positive sticky note comment.

Have Parents Fill Out a Questionnaire About Their Child

What does your child enjoy doing in his free time?

_____

_____

_____

What does your child enjoy about school?

_____

_____

_____

What does he dislike about school?

_____

_____

_____

In our book, *The Growth Mindset Coach*, we share a legend from Cherokee lore that analogizes the importance of honing your self-talk so well, it bears repeating here.

> *A grandfather is talking to his grandson about his experiences in life. He tells the son that he has two wolves inside him. One wolf is evil—it is greed, envy, hatred, arrogance, and darkness. The other wolf is good —it is generosity, hope, love, humility, and light. These two wolves, the good and the evil, are at battle within all people, the grandfather tells his grandson.*
>
> *The grandson looks at the grandfather and asks, "Which wolf wins?"*
>
> *And the grandfather replies, "The one you feed."*

Like the two wolves in the old legend, the fixed and growth mindsets are alive in our heads, jockeying for position. Just when your growth mindset is feeling satisfied with a hard day's work, your fixed mindset swoops in and undermines it by asking, "But was it good enough?" Here are some common examples of fixed-mindset self-talk people engage in, and how to respond to those messages with a growth mindset.

Responding to the Fixed Mindset

Fixed-Mindset Self-Talk	Growth-Mindset Response
"I'll never be as good as _____"	"I did better than I did the day before."
"I just wasn't meant to do this."	"I'm making progress toward my goal."
"I don't have what it takes."	"I'm not there yet!"
"This is too hard!"	"If it were easy, I wouldn't be learning."
"I am not cut out for this. Just give it up now! I am just going to embarrass myself."	"I can do this! I'm going to get a mentor, set goals, determine my limitations and obstacles that might get in the way, and then strategize a plan for getting the job done!"

Our self-talk can also be our harshest critic. Make efforts to make sure your self-talk is positive and kind. Instead of berating yourself for a failed lesson or a negative interaction with a student, speak to yourself as you would a student who has failed in some way or made a mistake—with love and compassion. Being critical of ourselves isn't necessarily a bad thing. We should reflect on our teaching practices with a critical eye, but we should do it in a way that is helpful, not in a way that attacks our value and self-worth. Here are some examples for reframing critical self-talk with kindness.

Reframing Self-Talk

Critical Self-Talk without Reflection	Critical Self-Talk with Reflection
That lesson was a total flop.	Teaching is trial and error. I can salvage the good parts of this lesson and improve what didn't work.
I snapped at that student; why can't I have patience with my students?	Everyone has a bad day. I need to apologize and move on.
Of course I wasn't nominated for Teacher of the Year. I'll always be mediocre.	Teaching isn't about rewards and recognition. It's about continually getting better and doing my best work for my students.
My students are so disrespectful; it's obvious they hate me.	Good relationships take time. I need to work harder to connect with my students.

Sandra tells us a story about how she once struggled with students who were working ahead on a group task, missing some critical pre-teaching. Finally, she snapped at one student who had worked ahead. The student had tears in his eyes, and she quickly realized her mistake. He had not worked ahead at all, she only thought he had. She felt terrible and apologized profusely to the student. She berated herself all day for her mistake and for losing her temper with a student—one who was completely innocent, no less. She shared the story with a few trusted colleagues, and to her surprise, they were far more understanding than she had been to herself. She heard things like:

- "I know how you're feeling, I've done that before."

- "You're a great teacher; everyone makes mistakes."

- "You apologized and owned up to your mistake. A lot of adults wouldn't have done that."

- "We've all done some form of that same thing; the important thing is you made it right with the student by admitting your mistake."

Sandra quickly realized that her harshest critic was her own inner voice, but it wasn't saying anything remotely helpful. The next day, she apologized to the student again, and he said, somewhat exasperatedly, "Seriously, Ms. M., mistakes happen. You need to let it go."

Often, we can be our own worst critic. As we said, looking at our teaching practice with a critical eye is a good thing, but being harsh and unkind won't help in the long run. Aim to speak to yourself the way you would an old friend.

OPTIMIZING SELF-TALK AND MANAGING MINDSETS

It's important to not only hone your own self-talk, but also to help students acknowledge the voices in their heads. In *The Growth Mindset Coach*, we told a story of a little boy whose conscience led him to confess a transgression to his teacher apropos of nothing but personal guilt. When his teacher asked him, "Did that little voice in your head make you come tell me this?" he got wide-eyed and asked, "How do you know about the little voice in my head?" Here are some strategies for optimizing self-talk and managing mindsets.

Use a Catchphrase

Studies have shown that coming up with a catchphrase can help athletes get their heads back in the game. In the same way, students who feel they are slipping into their fixed mindset can use a go-to catchphrase as a psychological cue to get back in the growth mindset. It might be something motivational like, "I know I can do this!" Or it might be a point of clarification like, "This challenge is helping me grow."

Name Your Fixed Mindset

Have students name their fixed mindset. When their fixed-mindset voice says, "You know, it would be much easier to quit right now," they could say, "Buzz off, Buddy!" right back at it.

Role-Playing the Mindsets

Help students prepare for dealing with fixed mindsets in others by having them write vignettes or skits and act them out. For example, students might write a skit with a fixed-mindset adult saying, "It's okay, not everyone is good at algebra," and a student responding, "I'm not good at algebra yet, but with lots of hard work, I will be."

Accountability Partners

Have students team up as accountability partners and pledge to help foster each other's growth mindsets. If your partner is buckling under the pressure of fixed-mindset messages, give them a growth-mindset pep talk.

Draw Your Fixed Mindset

Putting words and pictures to your fixed mindset is a great way to conceptualize it. This exercise will help students better recognize when they are in the fixed mindset, and once they can recognize it, it's much easier to control it.

Letter to My Fixed Mindset

Have students author a letter to their fixed mindsets from their growth mindsets.

***

Make sure that your students understand what self-talk is and know that all people have it. You may even give them some of these famous quotes about self-talk to illustrate that all people—even the most famous and successful among us—have a little voice in their head and recognize its power in dictating what we do and how we do it. We recommend giving students a quote to wrestle with, then ask them to paraphrase the quote and describe how they can apply it to their self-talk.

- "If you hear a voice within you say, 'you cannot paint,' then by all means paint, and that voice will be silenced." *Vincent Van Gogh*

- "You wouldn't worry so much about what others think of you if you realized how seldom they do." *Eleanor Roosevelt*

- "Trust yourself. Create the kind of self that you will be happy to live with all your life. Make the most of yourself by fanning the tiny, inner sparks of possibility into flames of achievement." *Golda Meir*

- "Confidence comes not from always being right but from not fearing to be wrong." *Peter T. McIntyre*

- "Argue for your limitations and, sure enough, they're yours." *Richard Bach*

- "You, yourself, as much as anyone in the entire universe, deserve your love and affection." *Buddha*

- "Our deepest fear is not that we are inadequate. Our deepest fear is that we are powerful beyond measure. It is our light, not our darkness, that most frightens us. We ask ourselves, 'Who am I to be brilliant, gorgeous, talented, fabulous?' Actually, who are you not to be?" *Marianne Williamson*

Make an effort to practice with your students how to turn fixed-mindset talk into growth-mindset talk. First, give them some concrete examples of what fixed- and growth-mindset self-talk sounds like. Here are some examples.

Fixed Mindset	Growth Mindset
When I have to ask for help or get called on in class, I get anxious and feel like people will think I'm not smart.	The question I have is likely the same question someone else in class may have. It's important for me to ask so I can better understand what I am learning.
My teacher gave me a low score on my presentation. I knew I couldn't do the work because I'm just not creative. There is no way I am revising it for a better score.	My score wasn't as good as I had hoped; I am going to revise my work and ask for help from my teacher.
I've tried to learn my part for the musical, but I just can't get it. I knew I shouldn't have tried out. I'm not talented enough to be on stage.	I am struggling to learn my part for the musical. I think I should try a different strategy, such as creating an audio recording so I can listen to my part rather than just read it.

Fixed Mindset	Growth Mindset
I came in last during my mile run. I'm not an athlete and I'll never meet my personal goal.	I came in last on my mile run today, but I didn't have to walk, and I shaved 2 minutes off my personal best.

Next, give students a specific scenario along with a T-chart to fill out that features fixed-mindset statements about the scenario. Ask the students to rewrite the statements in the growth-mindset voice. Here's an example.

> *Katie is a freshman student. She wants to try out for the dance squad, but she's only a second-year dancer. Most of the other girls going out for the squad have been dancing for more than five years. Here's the fixed-mindset self-talk that is running through Katie's mind.*
>
> *Those other girls are more experienced dancers than I am.*
>
> *There is no way I'm going to make the squad.*
>
> *I might as well quit before I get humiliated in the tryouts.*
>
> *I'm going to feel like such a loser when I don't make it.*
>
> *This is a waste of my time.*

Now, ask the students to devise some "comebacks" in a growth-mindset voice. Here are some ideas.

Fixed-Mindset Self-Talk	Growth-Mindset Response
Those other girls are more experienced dancers than I am.	They may have more experience, but that doesn't necessarily mean they are better.
There is no way I'm going to make the squad.	I have a chance, just like everyone else.
I might as well quit before I get humiliated in the tryouts.	If I try, I might make the squad. If I don't try, I definitely won't make the squad.
I'm going to feel like such a loser when I don't make it.	If I don't make it, I'll train harder for next year.
This is a waste of my time.	Doing my best to achieve a goal is an opportunity for growth and learning, not a waste of time.

Finally, give students opportunities to listen to their self-talk and reframe any fixed-mindset messages in the growth-mindset voice. Allowing students to spend time thinking about their thoughts and how those thoughts impact behaviors helps them become more cognizant of the role self-talk plays in the actions we take. Here are some ways to give students opportunities in the classroom to grapple with fixed-mindset voices.

- Journaling or blogging about ways to work through fixed self-talk.

- Identifying connections and/or "aha!" moments through conversations with peers.

- Telling stories of times they approached situations with a fixed or growth mindset, including what the outcomes looked like.

- Drawing or sketching a visual representation of their mindsets.

- Designing a comic strip story to illustrate steps for changing mindset.

IF/THEN GOAL SETTING

Another way to help students confront a fixed-mindset voice is to help them develop If/Then statements. This strategy isn't just useful for students; it can be useful for anyone who takes on a challenge and may have to deal with the fallout from failure. An If/Then statement helps people prepare for how they will respond to a difficult situation. In essence, it's planning to fail in a way that is productive. When big projects, tests, speeches, or other import-ant events are on the horizon, take time to help students develop If/Then plans. Teachers can also model this type of planning by engaging in it, too. In fact, If/Then planning for teachers is an excellent way to navigate the many difficult situations we find ourselves in each day.

Here's an example of an If/Then plan for students:

GOAL: I will learn how to divide large numbers.

IF/THEN: If I do not learn how to divide large numbers, then I will ask my teacher for extra help.

IF/THEN: If I do not learn to divide large numbers, then I will ask for practice advice from students who can.

IF/THEN: If I do not learn to divide large numbers, then I will practice 20 minutes per night for the next week.

Here are some sample If/Then plans that a teacher might employ:

IF/THEN PLAN: If my students perform poorly on this test, then I will review the data and reteach areas where they seem to be falling short.

IF/THEN PLAN: If this student acts out in class today, then I will take a deep breath and stick to my behavior management plan.

IF/THEN PLAN: If my request to attend this conference gets denied, then I will find an online option for getting the training.

METACOGNITION: THINKING ABOUT THINKING

To wrap up this section on self-talk, let's briefly talk about metacognition. We're including metacognition in our section on self-talk, because we believe that many of our metacognitive practices are rooted in the way we think—and talk to ourselves—about our own learning.

Metacognition is often defined as "thinking about thinking," though that is somewhat of an oversimplification. Metacognition can be better described as understanding and having control over the higher-order thinking processes associated with learning, such as planning, strategizing, and evaluating progress. It is a conscious approach to thinking and learning. When students are able to view their thinking and learning as a process of implementing strategies and evaluating outcomes, they can apply that learning to a variety of situations far beyond the immediate context in which they are working. For the metacognitive student, learning becomes less about the outcomes of learning (*I got an A on the test!*) and more about the process of learning (*X strategy contributed to my success on the test.*).

Metacognition is a critical process of growth mindset. It is all about managing our thinking and finding out what works for us. If we tell our students that their brains have the ability to grow with practice and hard work, we also must give them the tools that maximize that growth. Part of that is making our self-talk about thinking strategies visible. Start by making an effort to question your students about their thinking.

METACOGNITIVE SURVEY

Describe a time you felt frustrated learning something new.

_____

_____

_____

What do you do when you don't understand something?

_____

_____

_____

How do you connect new information to things you already know?

_____

_____

_____

Describe the feeling of learning something new.

_____

_____

_____

What felt confusing about what you learned today?

_____

_____

_____

Did you have any challenges in today's learning? How did you overcome those challenges?

_____

_____

_____

What could you have done better to improve your learning today?

_____

_____

_____

Another option is to use thinking stems. By completing the thinking stems, students make their thought processes about learning visible. This helps students consider the planning, monitoring, or evaluation of their thinking.

I know I'm learning when…

_____

_____

_____

I'm picturing…

_____

_____

_____

I'm wondering…

_____

_____

_____

This reminds me of…

_____

_____

_____

I'm thinking…

_____

_____

_____

I'm noticing…

_____

_____

_____

I'm feeling…

_____

_____

_____

I'm curious if…

_____

_____

_____

I'm connecting this to…

_____

_____

_____

Keeping thinking stems posted in the classroom is an excellent strategy for helping students respond to open-ended questions about their learning. It gives students a guidepost for how to begin speaking about their thoughts about learning. Here are some more strategies you might consider using to get students to think about the various aspects of learning.

Activate prior knowledge. Begin new tasks by activating prior knowledge. Help students connect the new learning with existing ideas. Show them strategies they have used in the past that will be helpful in this new learning scenario.

Check in on learning. Encourage students to articulate metacognitive strategies as they work through the process of learning.

This running dialogue about strategies that are useful or detrimental to thinking and learning will help them associate specific strategies with success.

Use metaphors to help students understand metacognition. "Driving your brain" is an excellent example we've heard. Tell students they are the drivers of their brains, and like drivers on the road, they need to employ specific strategies to help them get to their destinations. They may need to stop and ask for directions, take a different route, etc.

Understand strengths and weaknesses. When students have a grasp on the things they are already good at and those areas in which they struggle, they can use that information to their advantage. Help students identify their strengths as learners, and how they can use them as an antidote to their learning limitations.

Self-assessment. There are many self-assessment tools available. Use these to give students many chances to check in on their thinking.

Peer assessment. Sometimes we miss things about our own thinking or lack the framework necessary to employ strategies that might make all the difference. Creating an environment in which peers can offer non-judgmental feedback to one another can make a big difference in your students' success with metacognition. A teacher that values metacognition is one who positions students to be both teachers and learners of metacognitive practice.

Feedback. Feedback is critical in developing metacognition. Without it, students may continue on the wrong path, using strategies that are not serving them. By asking questions, offering advice, and providing feedback, teachers can help students more deeply examine their metacognitive practices.

THE POWER OF THOUGHT

In this section, we've discussed how the things we think and say to ourselves can make an impact on the way we learn. This is as true for adults as it is for students. We have the potential to help students harness the power of their personal speech to reframe their mindset, engage in positive self-talk, and practice metacognitive strategies. These all play an important part in strengthening our growth mindset.

TEACHER-TO-STUDENT COMMUNICATION

GROWTH-ORIENTED FEEDBACK

In this section, we are going to focus on teacher-student communication—both verbal and nonverbal. Specifically, we'll focus on how to offer growth-oriented praise and feedback, and the non-verbal cues that will support your verbal messages. When it comes to growth mindset, actions speak louder than words. Remember Dweck's assessment of the "false growth mindset"? Much of that comes from teachers claiming to have a growth mindset, but whose actions and practices demonstrate a fixed mindset about learning, intelligence, and talent. But before you make any big changes to the way you are communicating with students, spend a week mindfully monitoring what you are saying to kids.

Ask yourself…

- How do I most often praise my students?

- How do I most often provide feedback to my students?

- How do I respond to mistakes made in class?

- What do I do when students get all the answers right?

Once you have developed an honest picture of the language you are currently using in class, it's time to make a plan. Making a concerted effort to infuse your language with the growth mindset should not be viewed as a temporary solution. Our goal is not to help you pick up a few tricks to be more growth mindset-ish *today*; it's to provide you with the tools to construct a future built on a foundation of growth mindset. This will take time. You will mess up. You will want to quit. This is change, and intentional change is good.

There's a saying, "Don't let perfect be the enemy of good." This is particularly relevant here, because many teachers with whom we have worked realize they have been saying and doing things in their classrooms that may have led to fixed mindsets. They feel defeated. They want to give up before they start. But, don't! Don't let perfect be the enemy of good! Try to get better a little each day, and before long, you'll have developed strategies and routines that you can sustain over time. No one is asking anyone to have an unimpeachable growth mindset—heck, we write books about growth mindset, and still catch ourselves in the fixed mindset all the time. You'll never be perfect, but you can always be better.

THE POWER OF PRAISE

When we use the word "praise," what we are really talking about is a very specific kind of encouragement of effort known as "process praise." "You're so smart," is a commonly heard example of another kind of praise: person praise. Person praise focuses solely on personal traits and qualities of the student. The problem with person praise is that it sends the message that a student succeeded because of some inherent, inborn quality they possess (in this case, intelligence), rather than the effort they put into the task. Process praise, on the other hand, acknowledges effort, strategies, or actions that contributed to the success of a task. It sounds more like this: "You worked really hard at that," and sends the message that the amount of effort put into the task led to success. Let's look at some differences between person praise and process praise.

Person Praise	Process Praise
You're a natural at math.	These problems didn't give you much challenge. Let's move on to something that will really stretch your brain!
You're so smart.	I like how you used different strategies to figure out these problems.
You're such a good boy.	I appreciate that you cleaned up the art center without being asked.

Person Praise	Process Praise
What a brilliant pianist!	Your effort in learning to play piano was apparent in your recital.
You're a born writer.	Your writing shows you understand the value of word choice.

The same idea can be applied to constructive critique and feedback, as well. Person critique is feedback that blames a failure or setback on a quality of the person: "You're just not good at math." On the other hand, process critique focuses on the effort, or lack thereof, put into the task: "That strategy didn't work for you. What else could you try?"

Person Critique	Process Critique
You really messed this up.	This didn't seem to work out for you. How could you approach this problem differently?
You did your best, but it's just not good enough.	You didn't meet your goal, but what did you learn?
Maybe piano just isn't your thing.	Keep practicing. Every day you get closer to mastering this.
You're such a naughty boy.	You made a bad choice. What will you do differently in the future?

See the difference? Because person praise or critique is directly tied to a student's intelligence or some other personal quality, it can make them feel insecure about tackling challenges and potentially making mistakes in the future. Better safe than stupid, right?

When the teacher ties success or failure to effort, strategy, or action, the child is not evaluated globally, but just on that one thing—right here and right now. In that moment, unrelated to intrinsic qualities and personal traits, the student can better understand the connection between effort and achievement. In that moment, it has nothing to do with being smart or stupid; it has everything to do with perseverance and the process of learning.

"When adults praise students' intelligence after a student performs well, they send a fixed-mindset message: you're intelligent and that's what I value in you," writes Dweck in *Principal Leadership*. "When adults praise effort (or strategies), however, they send a growth-mindset message: You can build your abilities through effort."[11]

Dweck says that person praise, which attaches success to some trait or quality of the person, is fine when the person succeeds at the task. But what about when they inevitably hit a setback? If a person believes their success is attributed to personal traits, then those same personal traits must also be responsible for failure. Most people don't like to feel like rotten failures, so, the theory goes, the person will avoid challenging activities in the future to maintain their self-esteem. However, when the praise is attached to a process—an altogether separate entity from the person—the person's willingness to tackle new challenges and show resiliency in the face of mistakes and setbacks is not compromised by crippled self-efficacy.

Another type of praise we often hear in the classroom is vague praise. In vague praise, the person is given no specific indication of what was done that had value or meaning to the achievement. Specific praise, on the other hand, illustrates to the student specifically what was done that resulted in achievement. Teachers are often guilty of vague praise in the form of stickers, smiley faces, and "Good Job!" quickly scrawled at the top of the page.

Vague Praise	Specific Praise
You're awesome!	You're putting awesome effort in on this fractions assignment.
Good work!	Good work writing a detailed essay.
Well done!	Well done on your dance recital. I can see you have practiced a lot.
Great!	Great strategy; that took some creative problem solving.

If you feel uncomfortable with or unsure about coming up with specific praise, try using feedback stems. These sentence starters are a simple way to ensure that your feedback is specific and process-oriented. Here are some sample feedback stems:

- I noticed how…

- Look at how much progress you've made on…

- I see a difference in this work compared to…

- I admire how hard you have worked on…

- I can see you really enjoyed learning…

- Could it make a difference if you…?

- Have you considered trying a different strategy to…?

- You're on the right track here, but could benefit from…

Making an effort to focus your praise on the process, rather than the person, has the potential to foster growth mindsets among your students. It demonstrates to students that learning is a set of processes, not a natural gift available only to some. Your process-oriented praise will help support student learning goals.

BUILDING
RELATIONSHIPS

As we've said in both *The Growth Mindset Coach* and *The Growth Mindset Playbook*, any praise and feedback that you might offer to students will be far more impactful if you've taken the time to develop high-quality relationships with students. Often, it feels like kids need to know that someone else believes in their potential to learn, grow, and succeed before they can buy into it themselves. Here are some tried-and-true strategies for developing relationships with your students.

Morning Check-In

Have students sit in a circle and ask them to rate how their day is going so far (5 is great, 4 good, 3 fine, 2 not so well, 1 terrible). Pay attention to those students that give a low rating to the start of their day. Providing journaling time, drawing time, or one-on-one conferencing time will be helpful in moving them beyond any negative feelings they began the day with.

All-About-Me Bags

Have students place three to five items in a bag to describe themselves. Students share out the items and how each relates to them. Make notes on what the students share and be intentional in creating interactions that highlight the attributes and interests presented.

Create Agreements

Instead of a list of rules of what not to do, consider collaborating with students to develop a list of agreements needed to ensure the work you do together as a class creates a growth-oriented environment. Developing the agreements helps you set the tone with students and highlights what you will foster in the collaborative classroom.

Team Approach

Replace the pronoun "I" with "we." Make sure your language is inclusive. The team approach helps build positive interdependence in the classroom.

Be Transparent, Share a Story

Share an appropriate personal story with students: a time you struggled, a mistake you made, how you learned something new, a misconception, or a success you have had. Opening up with students and sharing your human side helps them better relate to you.

Q and A

Ask students questions and pay attention to their responses. This can be set up as a four corners task, where students answer the questions by moving to a specified spot around the room. Or, students can answer questions by sharing answers with two other peers.

Personalize It

Students create personalized items (name tags, poems, songs, time capsules, inventories, collages, etc.) to highlight their interests, likes, fears, hopes, etc. Appreciate differences! Understand how we all have limitations and strengths, and how those characteristics make up the people we are.

Positive Message

Share a personalized positive message with a student or ask a question by writing it on a Post-It: How did the meet go last night? I really like how you handled the situation with the group work yesterday. How do you feel you did on the ACT? Great questioning in class yesterday! You really got us thinking!

STUDENT ENGAGEMENT

When students are thriving in the nurturing classroom, they are engaged in the work of learning. But what is engagement? And what does it look like?

We define engagement as student connection to a learning experience evidenced by whole-hearted participation.

Of course, part of engagement comes from having high-quality learning experiences, but setting high expectations and developing relationships go a long way toward getting buy-in from students to engage in learning. Let's look at what an engaged student looks like compared to a disengaged student.

Disengaged Student	Engaged Student
Withdrawn and doesn't speak in class, even when asked.	Answers and asks questions. Interacts with the material, teacher, and classmates.
Hides face, sleeps, daydreams, or otherwise refuses to participate.	Listens attentively, offers ideas, collaborates with peers; integrates themselves wholeheartedly in the coursework and among classmates.
Does not complete class assignments, homework, or otherwise does the bare minimum. Performs far below potential.	Engages in work, puts forth clear effort, and values learning opportunities.

Disengaged Student	Engaged Student
Acts defensive, wearing proverbial armor to class as if they are going into battle.	Feels freedom to be vulnerable and takes educational risks; is not intimidated or fearful in the classroom.

Sometimes relationships—or lack thereof—can impact student engagement. Even if the teacher has set high expectations, the work is meaningful and challenging, and the teacher has made every effort to foster growth mindsets, negative behaviors can stand in the way of progress.

LEARNING GOALS VS. PERFORMANCE GOALS

ASK YOURSELF: Am I communicating to my students that I value learning or performance? Researchers examined "classroom goal structures" and determined students are motivated toward learning goals or performance goals based on aspects of the classroom environment.[12]

LEARNING GOALS: A goal that focuses on the learning outcome of a task.

"I will learn how to do long division."

PERFORMANCE GOALS: A goal that focuses on the performance of a task.

"I will get an A on my long-division test."

Here are some more examples of learning and performance goals.

Performance Goal	Learning Goal
I will get an A on my math final.	I will learn to multiply numbers to 20 with fluency.
I will get a 90% on my Spanish exam.	I will learn how to speak Spanish.
I will score three goals in the soccer game.	I will learn to shoot using my left foot.
I will beat the chess champion.	I will learn to play chess.
I will use the engineering design process to create the best invention in the class.	I will learn to apply the engineering design process in my after-school robotics battle.

As you may have guessed, learning goals are preferable to performance goals, because while performance goals simply focus on knowing enough to perform optimally for a short duration of time, learning goals focus on mastery. Unsurprisingly, the environment we create in our classroom influences whether our students are establishing learning goals or performance goals.

THE CLASSROOM ENVIRONMENT

In most classrooms, we see a spectrum of environments. We've found that students learn better when they are in a safe and nurturing environment that sets (and enforces) appropriate limits. We call this "the nurtured classroom." Let's look at what a nurtured classroom looks like compared to two other types of classroom environments we commonly see: the coddled classroom and the disconnected classroom.

Coddled Classroom	Nurtured Classroom	Disconnected Classroom
Mistakes are overlooked and have no real consequences.	Mistakes are learning opportunities followed by second (or third) chances.	Mistakes result in disciplinary action and/or loss of arbitrary points.

Coddled Classroom	Nurtured Classroom	Disconnected Classroom
The students love the teacher because he/she lets them do what they want.	The students love the teacher because he/she encourages them to challenge themselves and is responsive to student needs.	Students view the teacher as an authoritarian figure/ gatekeeper.
Teacher believes some students just aren't cut out for some subjects, and that's okay!	Teacher believes with effort and practice, every student can make achievement gains in any discipline.	Teacher believes as long as students pass the test, who cares?
Students are helpless and need to be closely managed through the learning process.	Students manage their own learning and are encouraged to take risks. Teacher serves as a facilitator and guide.	Students do what the teacher says; if they don't, they are non-compliant. If they do, they are "good students."

· Are you creating the conditions for a nurturing classroom? If students feel their teacher is too cavalier about their achievements or don't think they can handle challenges, or conversely, too focused on compliance and test scores, they may not feel conditions are right to engage in real learning, mistakes and all. The sweet spot is the responsive teacher in a nurturing classroom environment— one who provides appropriate challenges, sets high expectations, and responds to student needs. But how do you get there?

Researcher Robert Rosenthal, who studied the impact of teacher expectations on students, identified four factors that were critical in developing teacher's attitudes about students' abilities in any given classroom.[13]

ROSENTHAL'S FOUR FACTORS

Rosenthal's work revealed that when teachers set high expectations and demonstrated belief in their students' ability to live up to those expectations, the students had better outcomes. As with growth mindset, we must believe that student achievement is possible in order to help them achieve. Consider trying a few strategies in each of the four areas Rosenthal described.

Climate	Input
The teacher demonstrates behavior toward the student that is considered warm and familiar.	The teacher invests more time and energy into those students for whom the teacher has higher expectations.
Output	**Feedback**
The teacher calls on students for whom the teacher has high expectations, more often demonstrating confidence in the student to know the answer.	The teacher gives a higher quantity of responses with better quality feedback to the students for whom the teacher has higher expectations.

Climate

- Establish class norms so all students are familiar with the desired practices of the classroom, which has clearly defined procedures and codes of conduct.

- Use positive, appropriate physical reinforcement (hugs, high fives, fist bumps, secret handshakes).

- Offer students autonomy over tasks.

- Smile at and interact warmly with all students; avoid sighing, glaring, and rolling eyes at all times.

- Show interest in the personal lives of all students; this communicates respect. Inquire and connect to their backgrounds. Ensure student diversity is represented in the books, music, poetry, and current event topics utilized in class.

- Make strong eye contact with all students; teachers tend to make less eye contact with students of whom they have lower expectations.

- Make efforts to be in close physical proximity to all students; teachers may tend to sit high-expectation students in the front of the room. Avoid this practice.

STRATEGIES
Input

- Develop go-to strategies students can access. For example, in problem solving, you may establish an "Ask Three Then Ask Me" protocol.

- Give students clear examples of great work, so they know what you expect of them.

- Use the I Do, We Do, You Do (or gradual release of responsibility) method. This includes modeling through direct instruction and guided practice as you work through the learning process together.

- Involve all students in developing rubrics. Make sure all students are very clear about what is expected.

- Provide equity in time, attention, support, and resources; ensure that each student can access the tools he or she needs to succeed.

- Check in on all students as they are engaging in work to make sure they are on the right track.

- Be available equally to all students to answer questions, provide guidance, etc.

Output

- Allow students to coach one another to try new methods, research, review work, etc.

- Display work from students that shows improvement or hard work, not perfection.

- Allow students to engage in independent practice.

- Call on all students when asking questions, and give them equal time to answer.

- Ask all students for ideas and opinions; find positive ways to compel students to contribute.

- Give all students opportunities to practice skills.

- Give all students equal opportunities for extra credit, projects, and classroom jobs and tasks.

Feedback

- Offer "yet" feedback when a student struggles with a problem: "You haven't got it" vs. "You haven't got it yet."

- Avoid unhelpful feedback like "good job" or "nice work." Always avoid negative generalizations like "You're a bad kid."

- Provide effort-oriented, specific feedback as the student works through learning tasks and independent practice.

- Be specific about what you liked about the student work.

- Be specific about what you did not like about the student work, and provide instruction on how they can improve it.

- Always give opportunities for students to address feedback and resubmit work.

- Always communicate your belief in the potential of the student to succeed; reinforce achievement and positive performance with appropriate praise.

The TARGET system, first constructed by educational psychologist Carole Ames, looks at six aspects, or dimensions, of classroom environment that lead to either performance-oriented or learning-oriented classroom goal structures: [14]

Task

Authority

Recognition

Grouping

Evaluation

Time

Look at the charts on the following pages to learn more about each of these dimensions and determine whether your classroom is performance- or learning-oriented.

Tasks

Includes the type of learning tasks the students are assigned, and the rigor, engagement, and value inherent in the tasks.

Performance-Oriented Classrooms	Learning-Oriented Classrooms
Tasks are often considered too easy and not engaging to the students, and often include performance tasks (e.g., rote memorization and demonstration of math facts). Very little personalization of tasks.	Students work on challenging tasks that offer equity and variety in process and product, and are of high interest to the students. The students find meaning and value in the tasks assigned.

Authority

Includes the role of students as decision makers and directors of learning, and their role in classroom leadership tasks.

Performance-Oriented Classrooms	Learning-Oriented Classrooms
The teacher provides clear directives on tasks; there is little room for student input. Teacher is the leader of the class.	Learning is often student led; students are empowered to make decisions about tasks. Students are empowered to take on leadership in learning.

Recognition

Includes how and why students receive recognition.

Performance-Oriented Classrooms	Learning-Oriented Classrooms
Students are incentivized and recognized for turning in flawless work, following rules, and finishing work efficiently. Taking risks and developing creative strategies are not encouraged.	Students are incentivized and recognized for demonstrating effort, improving skills, and accomplishing learning goals. Taking risks and developing creative strategies are encouraged.

Grouping

Includes how students are grouped together in collaborative learning.

Performance-Oriented Classrooms	Learning-Oriented Classrooms
Homogeneous grouping strategies are utilized, including ability grouping; groups feature superficial collaborative efforts and underlying competitiveness between group members and among groups.	Heterogeneous grouping strategies are used that feature different learning styles, strategies, levels, and philosophies. Students encouraged to engage in deep collaboration.

Evaluation

Includes how the teacher assesses student work process and product, and evaluation procedures in place.

Performance-Oriented Classrooms	Learning-Oriented Classrooms
No equity in assessment and evaluation; evaluation often done publicly, with a focus on how students perform in relationship to one another.	Evaluation of students is varied and done in a private fashion. Individual progress is often assessed with a focus on improvement and progress toward mastery.

Time

Includes how a teacher plans class time and how time is used in the completion of tasks.

Performance-Oriented Classrooms	Learning-Oriented Classrooms
Time limits are strictly enforced, with very little deviation from the original plan. Students are not given variation in time limits to complete tasks, regardless of differences in learning place and pace. Quickness and efficiency is valued over mastery.	Students are encouraged to work at their own pace; schedule can be easily adapted to address gaps or allow for enrichment or remediation. Mastery is valued over quickness.

BUILDING FLUENT RESPONSE TO MISTAKES

Mistakes offer excellent opportunities to create a growth-oriented environment. Explicitly teaching students the value of failure in the learning process will help them connect to the figures they are reading about in their textbooks. Modeling the value of mistakes as learning opportunities will help students see their own difficulties as temporary obstacles to be worked through instead of as permanent dysfunctions or failures. Here are ideas for using mistakes as learning opportunities.

Use Process Praise in Responding to Student Mistakes

WHAT IT LOOKS LIKE: Give them specific feedback and critique on what they did wrong and ask them to identify strategies for improvement—focus on the process, not the person.

WHAT IT SOUNDS LIKE:

- "I like how you showed your work using two different strategies."

- "You really persisted and used a lot of mental energy today. Keep up the effort! Tomorrow, I want to share a new strategy with you. I think chunking this task into smaller parts might also help you conceptualize the learning."

- "What parts of this seemed challenging? Don't forget we are learning new things, so mistakes will be made. This is part of helping our brains grow."

- "What obstacles are getting in your way?"

Grade Less, Dialogue More

WHAT IT LOOKS LIKE: Ask yourself: *Does this need a grade?* Instead of putting a big red letter grade on an assignment, try handing it back with an insightful passage highlighted or with a piece of useful feedback. Get students used to the idea of working toward a goal, not a grade.

WHAT IT SOUNDS LIKE:

- "Remember, when we make mistakes and experience productive struggle, we are igniting our brain for learning."

- "This was my favorite conceptual mistake on this assignment. Let's talk about how it was a mistake why."

Read Aloud

WHAT IT LOOKS LIKE: Find a children's book that demonstrates growth mindset and/or fixed mindsets, read it to your students, and discuss.

WHAT IT SOUNDS LIKE: "Can you describe the fixed-mindset traits of the character? If we were to rewrite the story to give the character growth-mindset traits, what things could we include? Have you ever found yourself needing to reframe your thinking?"

Model Growth-Oriented Self-Talk

WHAT IT LOOKS LIKE: Don't be afraid to share your errors with students. Talk out loud about your thinking processes.

WHAT IT SOUNDS LIKE: "Today's lesson didn't go as I had planned. I had to make some adjustments because, _____ (technology didn't work, the class needed a re-teaching session, I wasn't prepared to answer the questions, or I should have…)."

Talk About the Brain

WHAT IT LOOKS LIKE: Some students need concrete evidence that this stuff really works. Dig into the neuroscience behind growth mindset. Conduct lessons and activities that teach students how their brains learn and grow.

WHAT IT SOUNDS LIKE: "Did you know the brain is like a muscle and the more you exercise it (with regular practice), the stronger it will become? Let me teach a little more about brain plasticity and the science of learning…"

Another great strategy for shutting down fixed-mindset behaviors, which are often present in response to mistakes or failures, is to rephrase fixed-mindset talk to be more growth oriented. In other words, if you hear a student say something that has a bit of a fixed-mindset ring to it, try to rephrase it in a way that fosters a growth mindset.

What the student says...	How you can rephrase it...
"I suck at math."	"You haven't got it yet, but you will. Let's look at what worked and what didn't with how you solved this problem."
"I am not a good writer."	"You are a writer-in-training. You think Shakespeare wrote *Macbeth* in high school? It takes practice to be great, so let's practice!"
"That was an idiotic mistake."	"Now that we've pinpointed where the mistake is, let's talk about ways to correct it."
"This is way harder for me than it is for other kids."	"You might not realize it, but every learner in this class struggles. Struggling just means you're learning."

MANAGING DIFFICULT BEHAVIORS

It's important to recognize that not all relationships come together flawlessly. Sometimes we encounter a student with whom we have a difficult time developing high-quality rapport. Situations arising from undesirable behaviors may dog the relationship, or repeat offenses may lead a teacher to write off his or her ability to effectively connect with a student. In our experience, there is a sense of helplessness that comes from being unable to connect with a student and/or control or manage his or her behaviors. This helplessness may lead to fixed-mindset responses, like blaming and avoidance. A strategy that may work in this situation is reflecting on the behavior and developing an appropriate action plan.

First, take time to ask yourself pointed reflection questions about the student.

- What are my honest feelings about this student?

- Am I projecting those feelings to the student during class?

- Do I give non-verbal cues that indicate my lack of expectation or care? (Eye rolls, smirks, sighs, etc.)

- What situations most often trigger negative non-verbal communication?

- Am I expecting more out of my student than they can give at this time?

- Am I irritated by this student because I am otherwise frustrated, irritable, or in a bad place?

- Am I dwelling on negative behaviors with this student that I often forgive in others?

- What could I do to alleviate my frustration with this student?

- Have I considered any possible reasons for the behaviors the student displays in my class?

- What does my student enjoy? Am I making an effort to engage this student?

Once you have an understanding of your feelings toward and responses to the student, you may be surprised to find that you are part of the problem, too. For example, if a student is constantly leaving in the middle of class to go to the bathroom, nurse, office, locker, etc., consider that the student may be finding ways to leave class because they don't feel engaged. If students are constantly talking out of turn or amongst themselves during class, consider that you may not be giving them enough opportunities to speak during class time. Of course, there is an expectation that students should abide by rules you have set in your classrooms, but it is important that you fully assess whether those rules are realistic or necessary. Consider the following scenarios and decide how both the student and teacher could make improvements.

Ms. Franklin only accepts work done in blue or black ink. Ryan turns in a paper done in purple ink. Ms. Franklin gives the paper a 0.

WHAT CAN THE STUDENT DO DIFFERENTLY?: Ryan could work harder to follow the rules.

WHAT CAN THE TEACHER DO DIFFERENTLY?: Ms. Franklin could be more flexible and give students more choice.

Anna forgot her PE uniform. Her PE teacher, Mr. James, makes her run laps the entire class as punishment.

WHAT CAN THE STUDENT DO DIFFERENTLY?: Anna could put a system in place to help her remember her PE uniform.

WHAT CAN THE TEACHER DO DIFFERENTLY?:

- Mr. James could keep spare PE uniforms or allow students to participate in street clothes, in an effort to be more understanding that students can be forgetful sometimes.

- If forgetting becomes a problem, he could work with individual students on a plan to improve their accountability.

Tanner is caught copying homework from a friend in class. Ms. Gomez gives them both zeroes and a day of in-school suspension.

WHAT CAN THE STUDENT DO DIFFERENTLY?: Tanner could ask the teacher for guidance, ask questions in class, attend a tutoring session, or try to grasp the concept or skill by viewing lessons online.

WHAT CAN THE TEACHER DO DIFFERENTLY?:

- Ms. Gomez could provide formative checks in class to ensure students understand the lesson and homework.

- She could allow Tanner and his friend an opportunity to redo the assignment or demonstrate their learning by creating a video lesson.

- Ms. Gomez could also help Tanner and his friend learn more about the importance of peer coaching, as well as effective ways to guide one another.

When Zara talks out of turn, Ms. Timons takes away recess time. Zara has lost 5 minutes of every single recess this week.

WHAT CAN THE STUDENT DO DIFFERENTLY?: Zara could write her thoughts on a sticky note to be shared at more appropriate times.

WHAT CAN THE TEACHER DO DIFFERENTLY?:

- Ms. Timons could create predictable times for Zara to share her thoughts or provide opportunities for her students to connect to their learning by conversing with their peers.

- Ms. Timons could help Zara establish goals and share strategies for agreements for talking in class.

- Ms. Timons may also consider giving Zara a set number of "passes" for talking out and reducing those "passes" as she demonstrates success using the strategies.

- Praising Zara on using talk-times effectively will also be an important step in helping Zara understand appropriate times for talking in class.

***

If you continually have negative encounters with the same student, specifically if the undesirable behavior is repetitive in nature—like interruptions and speaking out of turn—try this technique: First, observe and ask questions to help identify specifically when and how the behaviors occur. Then, develop answers and action items for solving the problem you've identified. Here's an example of what that might look like.

A behavior I observed...
Johnny interrupts in class.
A reflective question about this behavior...
Why does Johnny consistently interrupt while I'm giving a lesson?
A potential answer to my question...
Johnny needs personalized supports to help him adhere to this classroom practice.
An idea for seeking to resolve the issue I've identified...
I will work with Johnny to develop personalized hand cues to let him know when he is interrupting and when it is an appropriate time to share his thought.

A behavior I observed…
Johnny often falls asleep in class.

A reflective question about this behavior…
Why does Johnny fall asleep in the middle of class time?

A potential answer to my question…
Johnny has been living with a noncustodial parent since being evicted from his primary residence. He also comes to school in the same clothes, which are often dirty, day after day. The instability in his living situation may be affecting his energy at school.

An idea for seeking to resolve the issue I've identified…
I will alert the counselor to my observations. Together, with any other necessary stakeholders, we will develop a plan for when Johnny falls asleep in class. I will also start a dialogue with Johnny to find out what, if any, of his basic needs are being met.

Engaging in this kind of hyper-reflection regarding your interactions with a particular student may seem time-consuming. But consider that putting in the time to identify your preconceived notions about the student and the possible underlying causes of the student behavior, as well as acting to solve the problem, will ultimately help minimize the amount of time spent managing the student behavior.

SHAME-AWARE COMMUNICATION

So many of the fixed-mindset responses we encounter include an element of shame. Whether that is assigning blame to a specific person or critiquing some aspect of personhood when giving feedback, shame has deep implications for developing a growth-mindset classroom. Growth mindset, at its core, is the belief that your traits and qualities can be developed over time. But, as shame and vulnerability researcher Brené Brown said, "Shame corrodes the very part of us that believes we can change and do better."[15] When we shame a student, we are also diminishing his or her capacity for growth.

What does a shame-aware classroom look like? For a long time, classroom management has employed tactics rooted in shame. Here are some examples:

- A teacher has students pull a "red card" when they misbehave.

- Teachers often make phone calls to home about a student's behavior in the presence of other students.

- Students are ability grouped for reading instruction; all the students understand the "bluebirds" are the poorest readers.

- A student caught texting in class is forced to read the text message aloud in front of her peers.

- An administrator engages in gossip about a staff member.

- There are clear favorites, both among the students and among the staff.

- Staff members rarely accept accountability and engage in finger-pointing and blaming behaviors.

- Teachers routinely have students grade one another's papers or share grades aloud in class.

In the shame-aware classroom, teachers avoid shaming students by developing more empathetic practices. It's important to not only examine how you feel experiencing shame, but how you bounce back from a shaming experience. If you believe a student is experiencing shame, it is critical to talk about it. A classroom that can freely name shame and meet it with empathy, what Brown calls the "antidote" of shame, is a classroom that offers students a fighting chance against its destructive forces.[16] If shame is the feeling of unworthiness and being unloved, then when a student feels shame, we must work to bolster his or her sense of value and belonging through words and actions. Where teachers and peers work to fight shame with empathy, it cannot exist.

Here are some examples of classroom management practices that will help you limit shame in your classroom, as well as some common shaming situations you might see outside of your classroom and appropriate growth-oriented responses to those situations.

A student talks out of turn.

SHAMING RESPONSE: Write the student's name on the board as a consequence.

GROWTH-ORIENTED RESPONSE: Explicitly teach students when it is appropriate to talk and when it is necessary to listen. Create opportunities for sharing out daily.

A student is caught texting.

SHAMING RESPONSE: Force the student to read the text out loud.

GROWTH-ORIENTED RESPONSE: Ask them to put the phone away, and later, have a private conversation about the phone policy.

Students perform poorly on a test or assignment.

SHAMING RESPONSE: Announce how many students failed the test/assignment.

GROWTH-ORIENTED RESPONSE: Provide effective feedback and allow an opportunity for students who failed to redo the task.

A student violates the dress code.

SHAMING RESPONSE: Send the student home or force them to wear school-issued clothing.

GROWTH-ORIENTED RESPONSE: Provide them with a copy of the dress code and offer concrete examples of what school-appropriate clothing looks like. If it must be addressed immediately, assist the student in discreetly calling a parent for a change of clothes.

Students are mean to one another.

SHAMING RESPONSE: Call them bullies.

GROWTH-ORIENTED RESPONSE: Hold them accountable for their behaviors, but continue to offer love and support.

A student complains to you that a teacher sat her in a corner after she talked out of turn in class, and she felt embarrassed.

SHAMING RESPONSE: March into the teacher's room and question her professional ethics.

GROWTH-ORIENTED RESPONSE: Find an opportunity to have a dialog with your colleague about strategies you use with the student in your class.

You see a student make fun of another student for failing a test.

SHAMING RESPONSE: Yell at the student for shaming a peer.

GROWTH-ORIENTED RESPONSE: First, offer empathy and support to the student who failed the test, reinforcing the idea that failure is an opportunity for learning and growth. Remind the student of your confidence in their ability to build understanding. Secondly, ask the student shamer to engage in a perspective-taking exercise. Ask them how they would feel if someone treated them in the same manner. Ask them to reserve judgment of others until they make an effort to look at the situation from the other person's perspective.

A former student has been removed from the classroom and is now sitting in the hallway, in the office, or in a buddy room.

SHAMING RESPONSE: Give a look of disappointment, disgust, or frustration as you pass by the student.

GROWTH-ORIENTED RESPONSE: Make eye contact and give an empathetic (and genuine) smile. Later that day or the next day, check in with the student and mention seeing them. Ask the student if they want to talk about what happened. If they do, then engage in conversation that helps the student identify problems and alternative solutions. It the student doesn't wish to discuss the situation, then leave them with the expectation that you know they will be able to do better next time. Make an effort to remind the student of their value and worth.

A preschool student breaks all the crayons in a box.

SHAMING RESPONSE: Say "you're so naughty."

GROWTH-ORIENTED RESPONSE: Explain to the student the difference between a good choice and a bad choice. Explain that breaking all the crayons was a bad choice. Together, come up with ideas of what good choices look like.

EMPATHY VS. SYMPATHY

If you're not responding to a situation with a shaming response, you may be responding with a sympathetic or empathetic response to a given situation. Our goal is the latter—the empathetic response—because in a growth-mindset classroom, communicating with students with respect and empathy is paramount. Let's look at some common situations in the classroom, and the different types of responses they might invoke: shaming response, sympathetic response, or empathetic response.

A student fails a test they worked really hard to pass.

SHAMING RESPONSE: "You should have worked harder."

SYMPATHETIC RESPONSE: "At least it wasn't the final exam. If you work hard, you'll do better next time."

EMPATHETIC RESPONSE: "It stinks to fail when we've worked so hard at something. Why don't we talk about what you can work on for next time?"

A student is disappointed they forgot to turn in a piece of homework.

SHAMING RESPONSE: "Hopefully you've learned your lesson about being irresponsible."

SYMPATHETIC RESPONSE: "I'm sorry you forgot to turn this in, but at least you'll know better next time."

EMPATHETIC RESPONSE: "We all forget to do things sometimes. Do you want to talk about some strategies you can use to help you remember?"

A student is teased by another student at recess and reports the conflict.

SHAMING RESPONSE: "Don't be a crybaby."

SYMPATHETIC RESPONSE: "I'm sorry your feelings were hurt. Just play somewhere else and avoid that person."

EMPATHETIC RESPONSE: "It hurts when others make fun of us. When you're ready, why don't we make a plan in case this happens again?"

A student says he is feeling stupid after being enrolled in a remedial course.

SHAMING RESPONSE: "Work harder and you'll get to take classes with the regular kids."

SYMPATHETIC RESPONSE: "Don't worry. You're not stupid, you just need extra help. You'll be glad you did it."

EMPATHETIC RESPONSE: "I know this feels bad. I had to retake a class in college once, and I remember feeling a lot like you are now. Do you want to talk about it?"

***

If you make an effort to change your words and practice empathy in small ways every day, your actions will become habits over time. You will transition from "doing" empathy in your classroom to being genuinely empathetic. The same goes for growth mindset. We are all learners in this process. With intentional effort in our thoughts, words, and actions, growth-mindset behaviors, like offering growth-oriented praise and feedback, developing strong relationships, managing behaviors, and growing empathy, will become a matter of course in your day-to-day classroom. Remember, don't let perfect be the enemy of good—take small steps to improve each day, and give yourself grace and forgiveness when you miss the mark.

PEER-TO-PEER COMMUNICATION

PEER-TO-PEER COMMUNICATION AMONG TEACHERS

In teaching, it's easy to succumb to what some in the education community are calling the "silo effect." It can feel like our worlds are revolving around what is happening in our classrooms, specific grade-level teams, or content areas, and we fail to make connections in the school community with those on the outside of our established silos. In many respects, silos are a necessary part of the school structure —it makes sense to develop curriculum with grade-level or departmental teams—but when they impede fluid communication and prevent collaboration in the larger context of the school, silos can become a major problem. Ken Blanchard, a leader in organizational development, puts it best: "None of us is as smart as all of us."[17]

WORKING IN A SILO

First, take this silo self-assessment to determine if you tend toward collaboration with peers or prefer to stay close to your classroom.

I am comfortable with my teaching methods, and don't really want to change.	**Y**	**N**
When people come in my classroom to watch me teach, I feel like I am being judged.	**Y**	**N**
My most important job is to lead instruction in my classroom.	**Y**	**N**
My coworkers' personal and professional lives are none of my business.	**Y**	**N**
Unless there's a problem, I don't need to communicate with teachers from different grade levels or departments.	**Y**	**N**
I have little patience for teachers who overshare about what's happening in their classrooms.	**Y**	**N**
I don't go to work to make friends; I go to work to do my job.	**Y**	**N**
What other teachers are doing in their classrooms does not affect me.	**Y**	**N**
I wouldn't take teaching feedback seriously if the feedback was coming from someone outside my grade level or department.	**Y**	**N**
I don't volunteer to lead professional development, because what I'm doing in my classroom would not apply to others.	**Y**	**N**

The only time I see the majority of my colleagues is at staff meetings or school-wide professional development events.	**Y N**
When something good happens in my classroom, I don't typically share it with my colleagues.	**Y N**

Check out your Yes answers on this quiz. If there were more than two, you may be missing out on important relationships and learning opportunities. Teaching in a silo might feel like you're doing nothing wrong—after all, you're dedicating all your working hours to your classroom, your curriculum, and your students, right? Maybe not.

If you find yourself siloed, it's important to ask yourself why, because silos can be indicative of larger organizational problems. In their book, *Collaboration Begins with You: Be a Silo Buster*, Ken Blanchard, Jane Ripley, and Eunice Parisi-Carew outlines the five elements of his UNITE model for improving organizational collaboration:

Utilize differences

Nurture safety and trust

Involve others in crafting a clear purpose, values, and goals

Talk openly

Empower yourself and others

The following strategies are adapted from *Collaboration Begins with You*.[18]

Utilize Differences

Colleagues are able to optimize differences among staff through collaboration, sharing ideas, and valuing a variety of points of view. Not all teachers are encouraged to be the same, but they are encouraged to be open-minded and ready to embrace new ideas and best practices.

Nurture Safety and Trust

Colleagues feel it's safe to fail in the school. There is no anxiety over informal observations or sharing ideas because the established environment is one of safety and trust in which all voices are valued. Model normalizing mistakes and learning from failure.

Involve Others in Crafting a Clear Purpose, Values, and Goals

Colleagues are united behind a common mission. Values and goals of all team members are aligned in pursuit of achieving goals and fulfilling the mission. Find ways to involve others as you work to fulfill the school mission and vision.

Talk Openly

Colleagues can talk openly about successes and frustrations, along with best practices and new initiatives. An atmosphere of sharing and openness exists in the school. Model valuing the process of giving and receiving feedback.

Empower Yourself and Others

Colleagues who build relationships, share knowledge, and collaborate on new ideas empower themselves and others. Encourage empowerment through being a leader in the sharing culture and promote an attitude of knowledge is power!

RELATIONSHIP-BUILDING IDEAS

If a growth mindset is the belief that skills, intelligence, and talents can be developed, when it comes to teaching we must ask ourselves, how can our practices be developed? We can't always be taking a new class or attending conferences, so we must find ways to reach out to colleagues to bolster our own growth. Here are some relationship-building ideas.

Mentoring. You are always in the position to be mentored. No matter what, there is someone in your building who has something of value to share with you. Seek out that person! Don't turn down opportunities to mentor others, either. It's a chance to share and reflect on your best teaching practices, and you'll probably learn a thing or two in the process, as well.

PLC groups. Form or join a Professional Learning Community. If you're already involved with a PLC, try to take a more active role. Here you'll have many opportunities to learn from and collaborate with other teachers and share your learning about growth mindset.

Committees. Get involved! Ask to join a committee you are passionate about. You'll get the opportunity to talk to teachers with whom you have this passion in common.

PBL planning. Plan project-based learning units together as a grade-level team, or vertically and across the curriculum. PBL will allow your students to work on collaborative skills over the course of a lengthy project, and it will give teachers a chance to collaborate, as well.

Cooperative teaching. Co-teach a classroom with another teacher. Strive to collaborate, communicate, and learn from the co-teacher. This could be arranged as a long-term situation or as a short-term collaboration between classes.

Book clubs. Choose an education-themed book each quarter for teachers to read, then meet and discuss thoughts and feelings on the book. This strategy is sure to spark interesting conversation, forge connections, and inspire new ideas.

Interpersonal relationships. Communication with teachers doesn't have to be all "shop talk." Make sure to have cordial conversations with colleagues about their personal lives. Bonding over a shared love of a band or baseball team, or inquiring about family or hobbies, can go a long way in building a friendly rapport.

Interest inventories. At the beginning of the year, distribute interest inventories to teachers, and publish the results. (Interest inventories are questionnaires that ask about likes and dislikes; they are meant to gauge an understanding of your work styles and values.) Through common interests, teachers who wouldn't normally work together may forge relationships with one another, creating a more cohesive school culture.

Observations. Pineapple Charts and #ObserveMe are two examples of programs designed to extend casual invitations to colleagues to observe your teaching in an informal way. Opening our doors—and minds—to new ways of teaching has the potential to build relationships, improve teaching, and create camaraderie among team members.

Just as students can have an unproductive fixation on their "rank" in the classroom (Who am I smarter than? Who is dumber than me? Who do I have better grades than? Who has better grades than me?), teachers can have an unproductive fixation on their "rank" in the school (Who is the best teacher? Who am I a better teacher than? Who do the kids like the most? Who really stinks at teaching?). But these kinds of fixed-mindset fixations don't contribute to advancing the mission. Just as we seek to view our students as unique individuals with different sets of strengths, weaknesses, abilities, and points of view, so too should we seek to view our colleagues in the same way. Teaching isn't a competitive sport—it's a collaborative one. Building relationships and productively communicating with colleagues is essential to moving the ball forward together.

STUDENT-TO-STUDENT COMMUNICATION

Teachers are often hyper-focused on the quality and style of their communication with students. But communication among the students in the class can also contribute to fostering—or flattening—growth mindsets. Despite your best efforts to normalize mistakes or value progress over perfection, student communication—or the feedback students are receiving from one another—has the potential to act as a saboteur.

Modeling growth-mindset praise and feedback, along with other behaviors associated with fostering growth mindset, is essential to equipping students with the knowledge and language to help one another. Here are some strategies for teaching students how to use growth-oriented behaviors and language with one another in the classroom setting.

Normalize mistakes. Encourage students to develop an attitude that mistakes are learning opportunities; redirect students who struggle with this classroom value.

Teach constructive praise and feedback. Teach students how to give constructive, growth-oriented praise and feedback by giving examples and nonexamples, offering opportunities to practice, and redirecting when necessary.

Provide opportunities for peer review. It isn't enough to teach students how to give growth-oriented praise and feedback; they need to practice, often. Give students opportunities to practice as often as possible.

Value progress over perfection. Focus on rewarding effort in your classroom. Instead of saying things like, "On the test there were eight As and six Bs," focus on growth by saying, "On average, our class improved 32% from the pre-test to the post-test." This demonstrates a value on growth and progress, over good grades.

Student teaching. When students master a concept, ask them to help teach it to classmates who are still working toward mastery. Students who engage in teaching/learning from one another may recognize that learning is a process for each person in the class, rather than experiencing it only through their own personal lens.

Call outs. When you see a student engaging in growth-oriented peer interactions, let them know by calling out the behavior as a positive example. Taking this approach of pointing out authentic examples of positive interactions will convey the value of the demonstrated behavior.

ENCOURAGING PROCESS PRAISE AND FEEDBACK

As we know, the teacher isn't the only one in a classroom who delivers praise and feedback. Students are often tasked with giving each other praise and feedback. If you hear a student delivering person-oriented praise and feedback, take the opportunity to model process-oriented praise and feedback through rephrasing. You might even develop a list of person praise and feedback examples and ask the students to rephrase them, as you teach them to deliver constructive critiques to one another. Here are some common examples of person praise and feedback you may overhear from your students, along with ideas on how to reframe those comments into process praise and feedback.

Person Focus	Process Focus
You just don't get long division.	You don't understand long division, yet! Let's keep trying.
Tina is the smartest kid in the class.	Tina did well on this exam. You should ask her how she studied.
This is too hard for me.	Hard is good! It means you're learning.

Person Focus	Process Focus
Eric is great at this. I'll never be as good as him.	Let's ask Eric for some tips on accomplishing this.
I can't!	You can, but it will take time and effort.
I screwed up again.	Mistakes are a chance to improve.
This isn't working!	This way isn't working, so what else could you try?

Feedback stems can also be useful in the peer evaluation process. In using feedback stems, you essentially offer sentence starters that help students guide their praise and feedback toward the process orientation. These stems help students develop valuable process-oriented feedback to give to fellow students. Here are some examples of feedback stems.

- One awesome thing about your work is…

- I really like the way you…

- One thing that helps me is…

- This could improve if…

- My favorite part of this was…

- I noticed that…

Changing the way students give one another praise and feedback isn't going to be easy. For anyone, this shift in the way we deliver constructive feedback requires mindfulness and motivation. Help students with this change by being a model of growth-oriented praise and feedback. Help them see how much more useful it is for them as they work toward achieving academic goals, and encourage them to share feedback utilizing the same language, tone, and purpose with fellow students.

SCHOOL-TO-HOME COMMUNICATION

TEACHING PARENTS ABOUT MINDSETS

Teachers who seek to incorporate the science of mindset in their classroom would do well to remember that parents are an integral part of the equation. We must embrace parents as partners in the teaching and learning process. As Dweck says, parents who raise children to love challenge and enjoy effort are giving them an invaluable gift that will serve them throughout their lives. In this section, we'll help you develop strategies for showing and telling parents how critical mindset is to student outcomes, and what actions they can take at home to help bolster their child's growth mindset.

Many of our growth-mindset efforts at school can be dashed by fixed-mindset messages a student receives at home. Any teacher who has ever conducted a parent-teacher conference has likely heard some version of these common fixed-mindset messages from parents, who seek to take credit for, justify, or excuse away a student's performance by invoking genetics or natural talent (or lack thereof).

COMMON FIXED-MINDSET MESSAGES FROM PARENTS

- "Johnny's so good at math. He gets that from his father."

- "Meg isn't going to try out for the musical because she will never be as good as Beth."

- "Eric is so naughty; he never behaves."

- "Lilly worked really hard to study for the post-test and she only got a C."

- "It's not fair Ray didn't make the team. The coach obviously hates him."

- "I don't know why David can't get this. It was easy for his sister."

- "I'm not going to bother talking to the principal, she won't do anything."

- "Why is she in the smart reading group and my child isn't?"

- "My kid gets grounded one day for every missed word on the spelling test."

Despite our best efforts, fixed-mindset messaging at home can hamper a student's ability to truly develop a growth mindset in terms of their academic pursuits. After all, what would be the point of trying to become a better reader if you've already been informed you come from a long line of poor readers? If a parent invokes a fixed-mindset message in a teacher-parent interaction, make an effort to gently change the tone from fixed to growth.

If you have a student struggling to connect with growth-mindset messaging at school, ask yourself or the student about what might be happening at home.

- Does the child get in trouble for making mistakes?

- Is the parent quick to blame others for their or their child's failures?

- Does the parent help the child avoid challenging situations?

- Does the parent make excuses for the child's shortcomings or failures?

- Is effort and improvement valued at home?

- Does the parent celebrate when the child improves? Or are they fixated on perfection?

If you're dealing with a fixed-mindset parent, try to reframe fixed-mindset messaging to the growth orientation. Let's take the examples from above and show how a teacher might respond with growth-mindset messaging as a model to the parent.

Parent Fixed-Mindset Message	Teacher Response
"Johnny's so good at math. He gets that from his father."	"Actually, Johnny works incredibly hard in math. It is clear that he puts in a lot of effort, which has translated into top grades."
"Meg isn't going to try out for the musical because she will never be as good as Beth."	"Encourage Meg to ask for guidance from the director and ask Beth to assist her in practicing."
"Eric is so naughty; he never behaves."	"Eric is learning new strategies to self-regulate; it will take practice time and effort for him to build fluency."
"Lilly worked really hard to study for the post-test and she only got a C."	"Lilly scored a 27% on her pre-test and a 76% on her post-test. This shows how much effort she put into learning the material and the gains she made throughout the unit."
"It's not fair Ray didn't make the team. The coach obviously hates him."	"Tryouts can be tough. Maybe Ray could ask the coach to watch a few practices so he can get tips for making it next year."
"I don't know why David can't get this. It was easy for his sister."	"All learners are different. David might need to try a few different strategies before he finds what works for him."

Parent Fixed-Mindset Message	Teacher Response
"I'm not going to bother talking to the principal, she won't do anything to help us."	"You're the best advocate for your child. Let's come up with a few possible solutions to the issue and approach the principal with that information."
"Why is she in the smart reading group and my child isn't?"	"The best way to improve in reading is to practice at home each night."
"My kid gets grounded one day for every missed word on the spelling test."	"Instead of grounding, you might try having your child practice spelling the missed word and retaking the test."

SENDING GROWTH-MINDSET MESSAGES HOME

Another simple technique for a teacher concerned about fixed-mindset messaging from home is to include growth-mindset messaging in the form of feedback on homework. When the parent goes through the child's backpack at night, they may not pay much heed to a star or smiley face, but might stop to read a handwritten note. Try jotting down growth-mindset feedback on your students' work. Using a "feedback stem" or sentence starter can help these flow a bit easier if you're stuck.

I can tell that you…

> …studied very hard for this exam.

> …used some strategies we practiced in class.

> …worked collaboratively with your group.

One thing you could work on is…

> …increasing your response time.

> …identifying how you can respond to the situation using the strategies you have learned.

> …reflecting on the effort you put into each task.

I liked the way you…

> …used some study strategies we talked about.

> …made an effort to study a little each day.

> …helped your classmates understand this concept.

Many parents have anxiety about how their children perform at school. After all, we know that education directly translates to better lifetime outcomes, and less education is correlated with poorer outcomes like poverty, drug abuse, unemployment, and imprisonment. In other words, it's no wonder that parents feel the stakes are very high for their students to perform well in school.

An "F" on an exam might have an extra-anxious parent spiraling into terrifying scenarios in which their child doesn't make it into college and lives in the basement until the end of time. So, it's important for parents to understand that much of learning is making mistakes and retooling until you get it right. Think about how you incorporate normalizing mistakes and valuing failure in your classroom, and keep parents informed about it. If, for example, you have a resubmittal policy, make sure parents know about it. Little Andre might not care to resubmit an essay for a better grade, but if both his teacher and parents are encouraging him to do so, he may consider taking another try at it. Here are some more strategies you can use to include parents in your growth-mindset effort.

Tell Parents About Growth and Fixed Mindset

WHAT IT LOOKS LIKE: Do a family book study on *Mindset* by Carol Dweck.

- Attach an article on growth and fixed mindsets to students' take-home folders.

- Send a link to Carol Dweck's TED Talk on growth mindset to parents via text or email.

- Send home an easy-to-understand infographic about mindset.

Ask Parents to Help

Explain to parents you are using growth-mindset practices in your class and ask them to make an effort to do the same at home. Offer literature and resources to help them make this transition. Po Bronson's article "The Power (and Peril) of Praising Your Kids," archived on the *New York Magazine* website, is a great starting point.

Use Standards-Referenced Grading

As and Fs—and everything in between—can be very charged pieces of feedback because of the connotations associated with them. Instead, move to standards-referenced grading. Let parents know where a student has mastered a concept, and where they need improvement.

Focus on Growth

Make an effort to point out when growth occurs. If a student goes from a 55% to a 68%, point out the improvement, instead of focusing on the fact that a 68% is a D.

Give Parents Concrete Examples and Specific Things to Try at Home

Say…

- Try encouraging your child to take risks and tackle new challenges at school.

- Praise your child not for the ease with which they learn a concept, but for the effort that went into the task.

- Tell me if the work is too easy for your child, so that he/she can be sufficiently challenged in the classroom.

- Emphasize perseverance and effort in extracurricular activities. Make an effort to focus on the overall process that led to the success or failure, rather than the performance itself.

Establish a Partnership

Let the parents know that you need their help, and this joint effort is essential to developing their student's mindset.

MINDSET STRATEGIES FOR PARENTS

In *Mindset*, Dweck writes, "No parent thinks, 'I wonder what I can do today to undermine my children, subvert their effort, turn them off to learning, and limit their achievement.' Of course not. They think, 'I would do anything, give anything, to make my children successful.'"[19]

In our experience, if you offer parents tools to praise and motivate their children in a healthier, more purposeful way, many of them are willing to take you up on it. Because one thing all parents have in common is they want the best for their kids. One of the most important ways we can demonstrate the value of growth mindset to our students is to be a model of growth mindset. Tell parents there are many things they can do to model growth mindset to their child.

- **We all fall down.** Tell your child about a time that you failed and explain to them how you rose after the fall. What were the outcomes?

- **Quitters never win.** Talk to your child about a time that you gave something up and regretted it.

- **Winners never quit.** Talk to your child about a time you persevered, even when the odds were stacked against you.

- **Read between the lines.** Find storybooks, movies, or songs with growth-mindset messages to share with your child, and then discuss how the featured character or person used growth mindset to achieve their goals.

- **Actions speak louder than words.** Don't just use growth-mindset language; live the mindset. Acknowledge when you make a mistake and talk about how you're going to fix it. Normalize mistakes in your home.

One specific strategy we highlighted in our book, *The Growth Mindset Coach*, was sending home a growth-mindset message each week about an area in which the student might need extra growth-oriented encouragement from home. These little messages provide a consistent link from teacher to parent and don't take long to write. At the beginning of the year, talk to parents about strategies they can implement at home when they receive a growth-mindset message. Here's a sample growth-mindset message:

Stevie has found our new unit on long division quite challenging. He would benefit from regular practice and extra instruction at home in this area.

Then, offer parents specific strategies on how to go about doing this, such as these:

- Offer Stevie help on his long division. (If the parent is unable, find a friend or relative who can.)

- Encourage Stevie to ask the teacher for extra help before or after school and provide means for him to make it to these extra-help sessions.

- Provide words of encouragement as Stevie tackles long division (e.g., "I appreciate how much effort you're putting into learning long division," or "I had trouble with long division, too, but I kept at it. If you keep working at it, you'll get better.").

- Provide Stevie with extra help in the form of apps, work-books, or other materials that might help Stevie practice long division on his own when you can't work together.

Most parents don't have a degree in education, and, when it's presented in a non-threatening and supportive way, will often take advice a professional has to offer, if it carries the promise of helping their child improve. Think of yourself not only as a learning coach to your students, but to the parents, as well. Remember, you're not adversaries, but on the same team!

MESSAGES FROM THE SCHOOL

Growth-mindset messaging doesn't just have to come from the classroom teacher. In fact, coaches, instructional specialists, and other learning specialists should make efforts to let parents know that the entire school values growth mindset. If all the teachers are on message about the growth mindset, it can help create a growth-mindset culture, schoolwide. (More about that in the next section, The Whole-School Mindset.) The key is to help parents focus on the process of learning, not the outcomes. Give them tools to ask the right questions of their children that will demonstrate they value the process of learning over the performance aspect of learning. Those questions include things like:

- What materials did you use to build this?

- What strategies did you use to remember your spelling words?

- What were the study techniques you used in preparing for this test?

- How did you stay calm during the test?

- What previous experience helped you as you tackled this new challenge?

- What practice drills helped you perform in the basketball game?

- What were you thinking about when you were performing in the school play?

- How did your teammates help you be successful on that project?

Helping parents facilitate a conversation about the process of learning, instead of focusing solely on the performance outcomes, will infuse parent-student conversations with growth-oriented language. Explicit coaching on how parents can incorporate growth-mindset language into their praise and feedback will help make them aware of the fixed mindset and change for the better. It may seem awkward at first; parents and teachers alike will want to default back to complimentary praise like "you're so smart," mainly because it's easy, and it feels good and true in the moment. But taking a moment to craft authentic praise that focuses on encouragement of progress and process has the potential to pay dividends in the long run. As parents and teachers become more practiced and comfortable giving growth-oriented praise and feedback, it will become a part of their daily routine. Here are some tips for starting conversations with a child that focuses on the learning vs. the performance aspects of their daily lives at school.

Dinner-Table Dialogue

Develop a questioning routine to engage in at dinner time. Ask growth-oriented questions that facilitate productive conversation about learning and growth, like:

- What was the most challenging thing you did today?

- What was your best accomplishment of the day? And how did you achieve it?

Make sure to answer these questions about your own day, too! This modeling is key to developing growth mindsets around the dinner table.

Post-Game Debriefs

Lots of parents like to debrief with a child after a performance like a sporting event. When doing this, make sure your questions and comments are growth-oriented.

A sample comment would look like:

- I could tell those extra free throw drills are paying off. You hit all your free throws.

A sample question would look like:

- You didn't miss a line in the school play—how did you prepare for it?

Car-Ride Confidential

Experts have said that long car rides are the perfect time to engage in a conversation with your child because you have a captive audience. We think this is a perfect time to have a discussion about an area in which they are struggling.

Examples include discussing a challenge, a grade, an upcoming tryout, or a passion your child would like to explore.

- How can I help you?

- What are some things we can do to work on helping you learn this concept or skill?

- Do you know what it will take to help move you forward?

Bedtime Ritual

Bedtime stories on perseverance, mistakes, effort, passion, and/or growth mindset are gateways to having conversations with your child about growth mindset, effort, and struggle.

Make connections to the story by asking the following questions:

Did the characters encounter a problem? Did the problem get resolved? If so, describe the steps, obstacles, or challenges the character had to work through. Have you ever had to work through a challenge? What did you do to overcome it? How did you feel before, during, and after the challenge?

What advice would you have for the character(s)?

Did the characters approach the (criticism, effort, challenge, obstacle, or judgment) through a growth- or fixed-mindset lens? What are some examples for viewing it through the opposite lens?

Pick Your Challenge

Ask your child to make a list of challenging tasks/chores they have at home: folding laundry, cooking a meal, organizing a space, following multiple-step directions.

Next, set expectations on what needs to be done, ask your child to share some obstacles that might get in their way of completing the task, determine ways to work through the obstacles, and then let them make an attempt to complete the task. If your child makes mistakes while working through the task, be careful to pay close attention to your response. Try saying something like this:

- "When we recognize we made a mistake and attempt to fix it, we grow our brain."

- "How can we try this in a different way?"

Rather than saying:

- "This isn't even hard!"

- "Why can't you do anything right?"

- "You are messing it up on purpose!"

- "You're not even trying!"

- "You'll never make it in the real world."

ENCOURAGING GROWTH MINDSET AT HOME

It's important to find a way to keep the lines of communication open with parents. Teachers must create opportunities to facilitate the kind of growth-oriented relationship between parent and child that Dweck describes. By offering them information on the value of developing a growth mindset, along with tips and strategies on how to foster it in the home, parents and teachers can forge a strong partnership that has the potential to change how the student approaches learning challenges. Use these tools to let parents know what is happening in the classroom so those values and concepts can be reinforced in the home.

Texting. Use texting to communicate messages to parents from your mobile device. There are apps that help keep your private information, like your phone number, anonymous.

Newsletter. Use digital or paper newsletters to highlight ongoing learning. Use this opportunity for in-depth coaching to help parents try new strategies at home.

Social media. Set up a hashtag for your students (e.g., #Fabulous4thGrade or #SmithGrade6, as a way for parents to see what your class is doing via social media platforms like Twitter, Instagram, and Facebook). Share examples of students working on challenging tasks, and make sure your social media demonstrates the value of progress over performance.

E-conferences. Having a hard time scheduling a face-to-face meeting with a parent? Use Google Hangouts, Skype, or FaceTime to connect online. The more you can connect with parents, the more information and coaching you'll be able to offer.

Class channel. Give parents the opportunity to peek into what's happening in the classroom by setting up a video channel via YouTube or another video platform. They may be able to pick up some tips to use at home!

Polls and surveys. Constantly check for cooperation and understanding of your methods via polls and surveys. There are many free options, like Google Forms, for sending out polls and surveys and quickly aggregating results.

Classroom or student blog. Allow your students an opportunity to share their learning by blogging about activities, challenges, mistakes, and successes they experience in the classroom. Ask students to focus on the process of learning and specifically detail how they turned around a mistake in their communication.

Telephone. Sometimes, a good old-fashioned phone call can be just the ticket. Remember, you don't just have to call home when a child does something bad; you can call home with good news, too!

Handwritten notes. Jot down a quick note to a student sharing explicit process praise or a growth-oriented question:

- "You did a great job listening to the directions today and showing your work."

- "Do you think you did better on regulating your behavior today or yesterday? Why, and what did you do differently?"

Write a letter to parents with growth notes about their child:

- "Jack has been working so hard on his math skills. He's gone from averaging a 65% to 76% on daily assignments and has a great learning attitude. I appreciate the effort that he is putting in, and I thought you should hear about it. Go Jack!"

***

In terms of cultivating growth mindsets in your classroom, connecting and building relationships with parents can make all the difference for some students. As we said before, if a student is getting growth messages at school and fixed messages at home, it can become confusing. Share growth mindset with your parents and get them on board. Who knows? You may convert a few fixed-mindset parents in the process!

THE WHOLE-SCHOOL MINDSET

CREATING A GROWTH-MINDSET ORGANIZATION

"If you want to make small improvements in an organization, then you focus on changing attitudes and behaviors. If, on the other hand, you want to make quantum improvements, then focus on changing paradigms. Attitudes and behaviors will follow."— Stephen Covey, *Principle Centered Leadership*

Building growth mindset into the school culture is critical to creating a growth-oriented organization. Before, we said that organizations can have a growth or fixed mindset just as people do. Ask yourselves some questions about the culture of your school to identify if it is predominantly growth- or fixed-mindset oriented.

- Does the school culture encourage students and staff to embrace struggle and challenge?

- Do mistakes and failures result in valuable learning opportunities or punitive consequences?

- Do school-wide recognition initiatives reward effort or perfection?

- Is feedback used as a valuable tool on the path to improvement?

- Do people in the organization fear criticism or negative feedback?

- Are people in the organization compelled to compete with one another to be the most successful?

- Are people in the organization encouraged to seek out mentors within the organization and/or opportunities to learn from one another?

Sometimes, to identify whether an organization has a fixed or growth mindset, you need look no further than the school handbook. Consider the rules and policies being enforced. What kind of work is recognized? What processes are in place for improvement? Are the key components of the school culture best described as growth or fixed? Consider some examples of how a school organization might foster a growth-mindset culture vs. a fixed-mindset culture.

Growth-Mindset Organization	Fixed-Mindset Organization
The school has flexibility built into its policies and procedures with the understanding that people learn and grow in different ways. The school makes efforts to personalize learning, valuing the personal interests and passions of each student.	The school adheres to rigid guidelines regardless of specific situational aspects. The approach to learning is best characterized as "one-size-fits-all."
The school places a high value on growth, focusing on analyzing data collected by formative and summative assessment as measures of learning, regarding them through a lens of growth and progress, rather than performance and perfection.	The school places a high value on performance aspects of learning, focusing heavily on testing and grades as measures of learning.
The school empowers learners and staff to take ownership of their roles in the school. Learning opportunities, personal accountability, and an understanding of personal growth and progress are characteristic of this culture.	The school retains control of learning and has a top-down approach to learning, in which the stakeholders—including students and teachers—have little say in what is being taught and/or a lack of understanding of their role in the learning outcomes.

Growth-Mindset Organization	Fixed-Mindset Organization
The school values mistakes and failures as learning opportunities. Teachers are encouraged to innovate and try new things. Students are given many chances to master material.	The school takes a punitive approach to mistakes and failures. Teachers are afraid to try new things for fear it won't work out. Students are grade-driven and have little room to make mistakes.
School initiatives like restorative justice, for example, promote growth mindset by demonstrating the school values open communication as a path to understanding, learning from mistakes, and second chances	School relies heavily on tactics that may foster fixed mindsets like out-of-school suspensions, ability grouping, and performance goals.
The school promotes and celebrates growth. Students are provided opportunities to set learning goals, track their progress, and practice new strategies.	The school only recognizes performance goals, rather than learning goals. They celebrate those students who are on the honor roll or scored exemplary on an assessment.

***

In our presentations to faculties on growth mindset, we often engage teachers in a drawing activity that forces them into a situation where they might struggle with performance. We asked them to draw a sketch of their favorite animal to share with the group. Once given the task, we hear all manner of fixed-mindset statements coming from the group:

- "I hate drawing."

- "I stink at drawing."

- "I didn't know there would be drawing."

- "My favorite animal is a bear, but I drew a fish because I know how to that."

- "Wow! Nancy drew a perfect koala bear. I can't compete with that."

- "Of course the art teacher's is going to be amazing."

- "I'm the art teacher and I feel so much pressure to be amazing."

- "I don't want to share my work."

- "Tell me what to draw."

- "What's the point of this?"

- "I really don't care about getting better at art."

We also see non-verbal cues of discomfort:

- Rolling eyes

- Wide-eyed disbelief

- Sighing

- Defeated posture

- Attempts to cheat or trace

- Uncomfortable laughter

- Attempts to leave the room

- Withdrawing from task

- Avoidance

Most people aren't confident in their drawing skills, so conducting this exercise all but guarantees a few fixed mindsets will be triggered. Among teachers, who spend their professional lives being the expert in the room, struggling with a task can be an especially potent fixed-mindset trigger.

Now, think about how your school's administration reacts to problems and issues that have the potential to trigger fixed mindsets. Do they adopt the tone of the fixed-mindset teachers who don't feel comfortable drawing an animal by making excuses, assigning blame, being secretive, or relying on inflexible policies and procedures? Or does the culture insist that decision-makers react in a way that values identifying mistakes, taking accountability, and solving problems?

Here's the thing. If a cultural shift is what is needed, the message must reliably reach every member of the culture. So, how can administrators and other leaders in cultural change help initiate the shift? The first step is to adopt a litmus test, of sorts, that will help gauge the mindset of the school. For example, the school that promotes restorative justice over rampant out-of-school suspensions is operating in the growth mindset. A school that sweeps problems and concerns under the rug instead of acknowledging and attempting to rectify them might be operating in the fixed mindset. There are many ways schools can begin to make the shift to a growth-mindset culture.

Positive reinforcement. Instead of being reactive to problems as they arise, focus on creating new behaviors through positive reinforcement. Positive reinforcement is characterized by growth-oriented praise and feedback on what a student is doing well. Many fixed-mindset organizations have policies and procedures rooted in being reactive (how to handle a problem when it arises), instead of being proactive (establishing, modeling, and reinforcing the desirable behaviors and practices).

Take educational risks. Encourage teachers to take educational risks and embrace the process of learning something new. Remind them they don't have to be the expert before launching. Asking for guidance or seeking assistance, modeling how to handle mistakes, and facing challenges as learning opportunities are all ways we grow and learn.

Utilize complex instructional (CI) pedagogy. Complex instruction engages students by having them work together using multiple approaches to solving problems, which require students to help each other learn and meet the expectations. Tasks are open-ended and require a wide range of intellectual abilities and interdependence in the classroom. A significant part of CI is building routines and norms on how to work cooperatively. The end result CI is that students are taught they are socially responsible for the learning of the group and must craft thoughtful solutions to problems.[20]

Active learning vs. passive learning. Active learning promotes asking thoughtful and intentional questions, justifying methods or rationale, connecting concepts to one another, rephrasing problems, and providing opportunities that are rich and complex, with an expectation that students will need to collaborate with one another to collect multiple viewpoints and ideas to help them solve the problems. Passive acts of learning are more procedural and are done independently by following a set of processes.

Review policy and past practices. Review handbooks, policies, and unwritten norms to determine if they elicit growth- or fixed-mindset practices. Craft new policies, rules, and norms that promote growth-mindset messages.

Shift the culture around change. Administrators should share with stakeholders that change may be uncomfortable, mistakes will be viewed as opportunities to grow, and fostering a risk-tolerant culture will be necessary while embracing intentional shifts in culture.

Passionate professional development. Utilize professional development opportunities to help teachers engage in learning they are passionate about.

Observation/evaluation tools. Do the evaluation tools used by students, teachers, and administrators include growth language?

The tools should offer support for growth, and the feedback provided by those evaluating should include process praise and critiques.

HOW DO WE MEASURE SUCCESS?

If growth mindset is the belief that with practice, perseverance, and effort, people have limitless potential to learn and grow, then the way a school measures success should be focused on practice, perseverance, and effort, rather than performance.

Cathy is a high school teacher who said she kept seeing the same students get rewarded over and over. She said there was no surprise about who would be the Student of the Month, or get on the honor roll, or win the school awards. It was always the same kids who managed straight As. But, she believed, those were the kids who knew how to do school really well, not necessarily the ones who were putting in the most effort.

School initiatives designed to reward academic performance can be contributors to a fixed-mindset culture. But, how can schools spearhead initiatives that value those components central to growth mindset? Here are some ideas.

- **Let the data do the talking.** Collect student data and use it as a metric of growth. Share student data with the students and help them set goals based on growth.

- **Goal-oriented rewards.** Require students to set learning goals specific to them, and then celebrate together when the goals are achieved. Recognize those students who achieved personal goals. (Hint: Goals don't have to be—and shouldn't be—all about getting As.)

- **Share the vision.** Conduct school-wide morning meetings or assemblies that focus on growth-mindset messaging. Encourage students to face each day ready to persevere in the face of challenges, put in effort, and learn from mistakes.

- **Enlist student leaders.** Create a rotating commission of students in charge of recognizing effort and perseverance in the school. Many times, students will have a totally new and different perspective from the adults about those folks in the school who are working hard and making an improvement.

- **Revisit practices.** Ask teachers and other school stake-holders to go over the current school policies and discuss whether they foster growth or fixed mindsets. Crowdsource suggestions for changing policies to encourage growth mindsets among students, and follow through making the changes.

- **Create a mandatory class.** Success skills classes are nothing new. Develop a curriculum for teaching growth mindset and require it for students. Maybe all incoming freshman or middle school students will go through mandatory mindset training. Maybe the school can develop an online training for all students to complete. Whatever it looks like, incorporating mindset into the curriculum will convey that the school values growth mindset in its students.

For better or worse, much of the way schools are judged is rooted in the fixed mindset. It would be easy to succumb to the race for highest metrics for things like best grades, highest average ACT scores, or most graduates in the short term, but we must ask ourselves: Is that what is best for our students in the long run?

Growth mindset is a way of being. It is approaching problems with the belief that you can overcome them. If we want to foster growth mindsets in our schools, then our actions must match the rhetoric. Implementing policies that promote personalized learning or encourage standards-based grading are examples of schools demonstrating a belief in the potential of every student to learn and grow. Let us embrace the power of yet—the inherent promise that hard work will always lead us to learning and growth. Let us empower our students and colleagues to not be embarrassed by mistakes, but to recognize their integral role as a stepping stone on the path to success. And, as Carol Dweck says, "Let's not waste any more lives, because once we know that abilities are capable of such growth, it becomes a basic human right for children, all children, to live in places that create that growth, to live in places filled with yet."[21]

NOTES

1. Carol Dweck, *Mindset: The New Psychology of Success* (New York: Ballantine Books, 2006), 6.

2. Ibid, 16.

3. Ibid, 177.

4. Ibid, 245.

5. Ibid, 245.

6. Carol Dweck, "Recognizing and Overcoming False Growth Mindset," Edutopia, January 11, 2016, http://www.edutopia.org/blog/recognizing-overcoming-false-growth-mindset-carol-dweck.

7. Carol Dweck, "The Power of Believing That You Can Improve," November 2014, video file, https://www.ted.com/talks/carol_dweck_the_power_of_believing_that_you_can_ improve?language=en.

8. Christian Jarrett, "Brain Scans Can Help Explain Why Self-Affirmation Works," November 16, 2015, https://www.thecut.com/2015/11/why-self-affirmation-works.html.

9. Laura Starecheski, "Why Saying Is Believing—The Science of Self-Talk," October 7, 2014, https://www.npr.org/sections/health-shots/2014/10/07/353292408/why-saying-is-believing-the-science-of-self-talk.

10. Carol Dweck, *Mindset: The New Psychology of Success* (New York: Ballantine Books, 2006), 157.

11. Carol Dweck, "Mind-sets and Equitable Education," *Principal Leadership* 10, no. 5 (2010): 26–29.

12. Carol Dweck, *Self-Theories: Their Role in Motivation, Personality, and Development* (Philadelphia: Taylor & Francis Group, 2000), 18.

13. Robert Rosenthal, "Four Factors in the Mediation of Teacher Expectancy Effects," in *The Social Psychology of Education: Current Research and Theory*, edited by Monica J. Harris, Robert Rosenthal, and Robert S. Feldman (New York: Cambridge University Press, 1986), 91–114.

14. Judith Meece, Eric Anderman, and Lynley Anderman, "Classroom Goal Structure, Student Motivation, and Academic Achievement," *Annual Review of Psychology* 57 (2006): 492-493, doi: 10.1146/annurev .psych.56.091103.070258.

15. Brené Brown, *Daring Greatly: How the Courage to be Vulnerable Transforms the Way We Live, Love, Parent, and Lead*, (New York: Avery, 2012), 72.

16. OWN, "Brené Brown On Shame: 'It Cannot Survive Empathy," *Huffington Post*, August 27, 2013, https://www.huffingtonpost.com/2013/08/26/brene-brown-shame_n_3807115.html.

17. Ken Blanchard, Jane Ripley, Eunice Parisi-Carew. Collaboration Begins with You: Be a Silo Buster. (Oakland, Ca: Barrett-Koehler Publishers, 2015) 18.

18. Ibid. 147-148.

19. Carol Dweck, *Mindset: The New Psychology of Success* (New York: Ballantine Books, 2006), 173.

20. Elizabeth Cohen and Rachel Lotan, "Program for Complex Instruction," Stanford University, http://cgi.stanford.edu/group/pci/cgi-bin/site.cgi.

21. Carol Dweck, "The Power of Believing That You Can Improve," November 2014, video file, https://www.ted.com/talks/carol_dweck_the_power_of_ believing_that_you_can_ improve?language=en.

INDEX

ABOUT THE AUTHORS

Annie Brock, coauthor of *The Growth Mindset Coach* and *The Growth Mindset Playbook*, is a library media specialist and former English language arts teacher. She graduated with a degree in journalism and mass communications from Kansas State University and earned her teaching credentials through Washburn University. Annie previously authored *Introduction to Google Classroom*. She lives in Holton, Kansas, with her husband, Jared, and their two children.

Heather Hundley is director of curriculum and assistant elementary principal at USD 336 in Holton, Kansas. Heather has an elementary education degree from Washburn University and master's degrees in education and in school leadership from Baker University. She has served as a supervisor for pre-service teachers, guest lecturer at Washburn University, and instructional support specialist for Greenbush Southeast Kansas Education Service Center. Heather previously coauthored *The Growth Mindset Coach* and *The Growth Mindset Playbook*. She lives in Holton with her husband Matt and their three children.